THE PATH *to*
HOLINESS

BOOKS BY ANDREW MURRAY

The Believer's Prayer Life
The Believer's School of Prayer
The Believer's Secret of Holiness
The Blood of Christ
Divine Healing
Humility
Mighty Is Your Hand (edited by David Hazard)
The Ministry of Intercessory Prayer
The Path to Holiness
Raising Your Child to Love God
The Spirit of Christ
Waiting on God

THE PATH *to*
HOLINESS

ANDREW MURRAY

BETHANY HOUSE PUBLISHERS
Minneapolis, Minnesota

The Path to Holiness
by Andrew Murray

Copyright © 1984, 2001
Bethany House Publishers

Edited and updated for today's reader by Nancy Renich.
Previously published under the titles *Holy in Christ* and
The Believer's Secret of Holiness

Cover design: The Office of Bill Chiaravalle

Published by Bethany House Publishers
A Ministry of Bethany Fellowship International
11400 Hampshire Avenue South
Bloomington, Minnesota 55438
www.bethanyhouse.com

Printed in the United States of America by
Bethany Press International, Bloomington, Minnesota 55438

Library of Congress Cataloging-in-Publication Data

Murray, Andrew, 1828-1917.
    The path to holiness / by Andrew Murray.
       p.   cm.
Rev. ed. of: The believer's secret of holiness, formerly titled Holy in Christ.
1984.
    ISBN 0-7642-2561-8 (pbk.)
    1. Holiness. I. Murray, Andrew, 1828-1917. Holy in Christ. II. Title.
BT767 .M955 2001
234'.8—dc21   2001003783

ANDREW MURRAY was born in South Africa in 1828. After receiving his education in Scotland and Holland, he returned to South Africa and spent many years as both pastor and missionary. He was a staunch advocate of biblical Christianity, and is best known for his many devotional books.

Preface

No word in Scripture is more distinctly divine in its origin and meaning than the word *holy*. No other word leads us higher into the mystery of deity or deeper into the privilege and blessedness of God's children. Yet few Christians have ever studied or fully comprehended the word.

Many praise God that in recent years an emphasis on holiness has spread through many churches and Christian circles with deeper conviction than ever before. But so much is still lacking. Multitudes of believing Christians have only a vague concept of what holiness is. Even among those who seek to know it, few have learned to come to God's Word and to God himself to be taught. He alone can reveal this part of the mystery of Christ and of himself. To many, holiness has simply been a general expression for a deeper Christian life, without much thought about all that the term really means.

In writing this book, my objective has been to discover in what sense God uses the term so that it may mean to us what it means to Him. I have tried to trace the word through some of the passages of Scripture where it occurs to learn what God's holiness is, and what ours is to be, and to find out how we may attain to it. I wanted to point out how many and varied are the elements that make up true holiness as the divine expression of the Christian life in all its fullness and perfection. At the same time I have tried to emphasize the wonderful unity and simplicity there is in holiness as centered in the person of Jesus. As I got into this study, I realized what an awesome task I had undertaken in offering to guide others even to the outer courts of the holy place of the Most High. The difficulty of the task convinced me how much it was needed.

Some may be disappointed in what I have to say. They may have heard that entrance into a life of holiness is only a step taken by faith. They are seeking the secret to a quick resolution. They will have difficulty understanding that the answer does not come to those who seek holiness in and of itself but rather to those who seek Jesus above all else. Others imagine that all they need to know of holiness and the way to it is found in a few simple lessons—easy to grasp, to remember, and to practice. They will not find this approach in my book.

There is such a thing as an experience of Pentecost for the disciple of Jesus, but it comes to the one who has forsaken all to follow Jesus only, and in so doing has allowed the Master to reprove and instruct. There are often revelations of Christ as Savior from sin both in the place of private prayer and in the congregating of God's people, but these revelations are given to those for whom they have been prepared and for those who have been prepared to receive them. We all must learn to trust in Jesus and rejoice in Him, even though our experience may not be what we would like it to be. He will make us holy. Whether we have entered the blessed life of faith in Jesus as our sanctification or we are still longing for it, we still need one thing: the simple, believing, and obedient acceptance of every word that God has spoken.

It has been my desire to help others to trace the wonderful revelation of God's holiness through the ages as recorded in His Word. It has also been my continual prayer that God would use what is written to increase in His children the conviction that we must be holy, and then how we can attain that holiness in Christ. May He stir us all to cry unto Him day and night for a visitation of the Spirit and the power of holiness upon His people.

Andrew Murray
Wellington, South Africa
November 16, 1887

Contents

Chapter 1

God's Call to Holiness

But just as he who called you is holy, so be holy in all you do;
for it is written: "Be holy, because I am holy."

1 Peter 1:15–16

The call of God is the manifestation in time of His purpose in eternity: "Those he predestined, he also called" (Romans 8:30). Believers are the "called according to his purpose" (Romans 8:28). In His call He reveals to us what His thoughts and His will are concerning us and what the life is to which He invites us. He makes clear to us what the hope of our calling is, and as we spiritually apprehend and enter into this, our life on earth will be the reflection of His purpose for us in eternity.

Scripture uses more than one word to indicate the object or aim of our calling, but none more frequently than what Peter speaks of in our text: God has called us to be holy as He is holy. Paul addresses believers twice as "called to be saints [holy]" (Romans 1:7; 1 Corinthians 1:2). "For God did not call us," he says, "to be impure, but to live a holy life" (1 Thessalonians 4:7). When he writes, "The God of peace, sanctify you through and through," he adds, "The one who calls you is faithful and he will do it" (1 Thessalonians 5:23–24). The calling itself is spoken of as "a holy calling." The eternal purpose, of which the calling is the outcome, is also continually connected with holiness as its aim. "He chose us in him . . . to be holy and blameless in his sight" (Ephesians 1:4). "From the beginning God chose you to be saved through the sanctifying work of the Spirit" (2 Thessalonians 2:13). "Chosen according to the foreknowledge of God the Father, through the sanctifying work of the Spirit" (1 Peter 1:2). The call is the unveiling of the purpose that the Father from eternity had set His heart upon: that we should be holy.

Without doubt, to know what God has called us to is of infinite importance. To misunderstand here could be fatal. You may have heard that God calls you to salvation or to happiness, to receive pardon or to obtain heaven. But have you ever noticed that all these were subordinate to His main purpose? It is to "salvation through sanctification"; to holiness first and foremost as the element in which salvation and heaven are to be found. The complaints of many Christians as to a lack of joy and strength, of failure and lack of growth, are due to the fact that they have not given holiness the place that God gives it.

No wonder Paul, when he spoke to the Ephesians about being "chosen to be holy," prayed for the spirit of wisdom and revelation in the knowledge of God to be given to each believer that he might know the hope to which he has been called (Ephesians 1:17–18). Let all of us who now see to what we are called pray this prayer and ask God to show us that just as He who called us is holy, so we are to be also. Our calling, before and above everything else, is to holiness. Let us ask Him to show us what holiness is: first His, and then ours; to show us how He has set His heart upon it as the one thing He wants to see in us: His own image and likeness. Oh, that God by His Spirit would teach all of us what this calling means! It is easy to conceive what an influence it would have.

"Just as he who called you is holy, so be holy in all you do" (1 Peter 1:15). This call of God shows us the true motive behind His command: "Be holy, because I am holy" (1 Peter 1:16). It is as if God said, "Holiness is my glory: without it you cannot see me or enjoy me; there is nothing higher to be had. I invite you to share my likeness." Does this attract you and move you deeply—the hope of being partakers of His holiness? There is nothing better He could offer you. Shouldn't we cry to God to show us the glory of His holiness, that our souls may be made willing to give everything to respond to this wonderful call?

His call also shows the nature of true holiness. To be holy is to be Godlike, to have a disposition, a will, a character like God. The thought almost looks like blasphemy, until we listen again: "He chose us in him . . . to be holy" (Ephesians 1:4). In Christ the holiness of God appeared in a human life, in His own life here on earth. We have the holiness of the Invisible One translated into the forms of human life and conduct. To be Christlike is to be Godlike; to be Christlike is to be holy as God is holy.

The call equally reveals the power of holiness. "There is none holy but the Lord"; there is no holiness but what He has, or rather what He is and shares. The quality is not something we do or attain by our own power: it is the communication of the divine life, the inbreathing of the divine nature, the power of the divine presence resting on us. And our power to become holy is to be found in the call of God: the Holy One calls us to himself that He may make us holy by possessing himself. He not only says, "I am holy," but "I am the Lord, who makes you holy" (Leviticus 22:32). Because the call comes from the God of infinite power and love, we may have confidence that we can be holy.

The call no less reveals the standard of holiness. There is not one standard for God and another for man. The nature of light is the same whether we see it in the sun or in a candle; the nature of holiness remains unchanged whether it dwells in God or in man. The Lord Jesus could say nothing less than "Be perfect, therefore, as your heavenly Father is perfect" (Matthew 5:48). When God calls us to holiness, He calls us to himself and His own life. The more carefully we listen to His voice and let the fact sink into our hearts, the more will all human standards fall away and only His words remain.

The call shows us the path of holiness. The calling of God is one of efficacy, an effectual calling. Listen to Him and with divine power the call will work what it offers. He calls the things that are not as though they were. His call gives life to the dead and holiness to those whom He has made alive. He calls us to listen as He speaks of His holiness, and of ours like His. He calls us to himself, to study, to fear, to love, to claim His holiness. He calls us to Christ, in whom divine holiness became human holiness, to see and admire, to desire and accept what is all for us. He calls us to the indwelling and the teaching of the Spirit of holiness, to yield ourselves that He may bring home to us and breathe within us what is ours in Christ. Believer, listen to God calling you to holiness; come and learn what His holiness is, what yours is, and what it should be.

Be silent and listen. When God called Abraham, he answered, "Here am I" (Genesis 22:1). When God called Moses from the bush, he answered, "Here am I" (Exodus 3:4) and hid his face, for he was afraid to look upon God. God is calling you to himself, the Holy One, that He may make you holy. Let your whole soul answer, "Here am I, Lord! Speak to me. Show yourself to me." As you listen, the voice will be clear: "Be holy, as I am holy. Be holy, for I am holy." You will hear a voice coming out of eternity, from the council chamber of redemption. You will hear a voice from heaven, the Creator making the seventh day holy for man whom He had created, and saying, "Be holy." You will hear the voice from Sinai amid thunder and lightning, and still it is the same: "Be holy, as I am holy." You will hear a voice from Calvary: "Be holy, for I am holy."

Child of God, have you ever heard this call from God? Shouldn't we confess that happiness has been to us more than holiness, and salvation more than sanctification? But it is not too late to redeem the error. Listen to the voice that calls, draw close, and find out what holiness is, or better, find out and know Him who is the Holy One. If the first approach to Him fills us with shame and confusion, makes us fear and hold back, let us still listen to the voice that tells us to be holy, as He is holy. "The one who calls you is faithful and he will do it" (1 Thessalonians 5:24). All our fears and questions will be met by this One who has revealed His holiness with one purpose in view: that we might share it with Him. As we yield ourselves in the deep quietness of our soul to listen to the voice that calls us, it will awaken within us a new desire and strong faith to be holy.

O Lord, the only Holy One, you have called us to be holy, even as you are holy! Lord, how can we, unless you reveal to us your holiness? Show us how you are holy, how holy you are, and what your holiness is, that we may know how we are to be holy and how holy we are to be. And when the sight of you shows us how unholy we are, teach us that you make those partakers of your own holiness who come to you for it.

O God, we come to you, the Holy One. It is in knowing and finding and having you that the soul finds holiness. We come to beseech you to burn into our heart that the one object of your calling us and of our coming to you is holiness. You would have us be like yourself, partakers of your holiness. If ever our heart fears that this is too high to attain or rests content with a salvation less than holiness, blessed God, let us hear your voice calling again, "Be holy, for I am holy." Let that call be our motivation and our strength, because faithful is He that calls, who also will do it. Let that call mark our standard and our path. Let our life be such as you are able to make it.

Personal Application

1. Let me press upon every reader of this book that if it is to help him in the pursuit of holiness, he must begin with God himself.

You must go to Him who calls you. It is only in the personal revelation of God to you as He speaks, "I am holy," that the command "Be holy" can have life or power.

2. Remember, as a believer you have already accepted God's call, even though you did not fully understand it. Let it be a settled matter that whatever you see to be the meaning of the call, you will at once accept and carry out. If God calls you to be holy, then you will be holy.

3. Take a firm grasp of the Word: "The God of peace sanctify you through and through. . . . The one who calls you is faithful and he will do it."

4. Be still and listen to your Father calling you. Ask for and count upon the Holy Spirit, the Spirit of holiness, to open your heart to understand this holy calling. And then speak boldly your answer to this call.

Chapter 2

God's Provision for Holiness

To those sanctified in Christ Jesus and called to be holy.

1 Corinthians 1:2

To all the saints [holy ones] in Christ Jesus at Philippi. . . . Greet all the saints [holy ones] in Christ Jesus.

Philippians 1:1; 4:21

Holy and *in Christ* are perhaps the most wonderful words in all the Bible.

Holy is a word of unfathomable meaning. Even seraphs utter it with veiled faces. *Holy* is the word in which all God's perfections center and of which His glory is but the pouring forth. *Holy* is the word that reveals the purpose with which God from eternity thought of humankind and foretells our highest glory in the coming eternity—to be partakers of God's holiness!

In Christ—here all the wisdom and love of God are unveiled: the Father giving His Son to be one with us; the Son dying on the cross to make us one with Him; the Holy Spirit of the Father dwelling in us to establish and maintain that union! *In Christ* is a summary of what redemption has done and of the inconceivably blessed life in which the child of God is permitted to dwell. *In Christ* is the one lesson we have to study on earth, God's one answer to all our needs and prayers and the guarantee and foretaste of eternal glory.

What wealth of meaning and blessing when the words are combined: *holy in Christ.* Here is God's provision for our holiness, God's response to our question "How can we be holy?" When we hear the call "Be holy, even as I am holy," it seems as if there is, and ever must be, a great gulf between the holiness of God and that of humankind. But *in Christ* is the bridge that spans the gulf—or better, His fullness has filled it up.

In Christ God and humankind meet. There the holiness of God has found us and made us its own, has become human and can indeed become ours. To the anxious cries and the heart-yearnings of thousands of thirsty souls who have believed in Jesus and yet do not know how to be holy, here is God's answer: *You are holy in Christ Jesus.* Only listen to these words and believe. Repeat them, a thousand times, until God's light shines, until your heart is filled with joy and love and the words echo back: Now I see it. I *am* holy in Christ—I am made holy in Christ Jesus!

As we study these wonderful words, remember that only God himself can reveal to us what holiness truly is. Let us fear our own thoughts and crucify our own wisdom. Let us yield ourselves to receive in the power of the life of God himself, working in us by the Holy Spirit, that which is deeper and truer than the mind can fathom—Christ himself as our holiness. Depending upon the teaching of the Spirit of holiness, let us simply accept what Scripture sets before us. The revelation of the Holy One of old was a very slow and gradual one, so now let us, step by step, patiently follow the path of the shining light through the Word. More and more it will shine unto the perfect day.

First, we will study the word *holy* in the Old Testament. In Israel, as the holy people—the type of us who now are holy in Christ—we will see to what degree God sought to work into their very constitution an understanding of what He would have them to be. In the law, we will see how the word *holy* is the key to the redemption for which it was meant to serve and prepare. In the prophets we see the holiness of God revealed as the source from which the coming redemption would spring. They speak not so much of holiness as of the Holy One, who in redeeming love and saving righteousness would make himself known as the God of His people.

When the depths of meaning in the word begin to open, and the deep need of its blessing is shown in the Old Testament, we must go to the New to find how that need was fulfilled. In Christ, the Holy One of God, divine holiness will be found in human life and in human nature. In Him human will is made perfect and through obedience is developed into complete union with the will of God. In His sacrifice on the cross, that holy nature yielded itself to death so that like seed corn, through death it might live again and reproduce itself in us.

The Spirit of God's holiness is given from the throne and represents, reveals, and communicates the unseen Christ. In this gift the holy life of Christ descends and takes possession of His people, and they become one with Him. Just as the Old Testament had no higher word than *holy*, the New has none deeper than *in Christ*. Being in Him, abiding in Him, being rooted in Him, growing up in Him and into Him in all things are all divine expressions in which the wonderful and complete oneness between us and our Savior is brought as near to us as is possible through human language.

The Old Testament taught us what *holy* means. The New what *in Christ* means. In the Word of God, which unites the two expressions, we have the most complete summary of the great redemption God's love provided. The everlasting certainty, the wonderful sufficiency, the infinite efficacy of the holiness that God has prepared for us in His Son are all revealed in the blessed phrase *holy in Christ*.

"To all the saints [holy ones] in Christ Jesus . . ." (Philippians 1:1). In the language of the Holy Spirit, this is the name believers bear in Scripture. That we are holy in Christ is not merely a statement of doctrine. It is not a deep theological discussion to which we are invited, but the voice from the depths of God's loving heart addressing His beloved children. It is the name by which the Father calls His children. That name tells us of God's provision for our holiness. It is a revelation of what God has given us and of what we already are, of what God waits to work in us and what can be ours in personal, practical possession. That name, gratefully accepted, joyfully confessed, trustfully pleaded, will be the pledge and power of our attainment of holiness.

We will find that all our study and all God's teaching is comprised of three great lessons: The first is a revelation: "I am holy"; the second a command: "Be holy"; and the third a gift, the link between the two: "You are holy in Christ."

First comes the revelation "I am holy." Our study must be done on bended knee, in the spirit of worship and deep humility. If we are to know what *holy* means, God must reveal himself to us. The deep unholiness of our nature and all that is of that nature must be shown to us. Together with Moses and Isaiah, as the Holy One revealed himself to them, we must fear and tremble. We must confess how utterly unfit we are for the revelation or the fellowship of God without the cleansing of fire. Conscious of our utter impotence to know God through our own wisdom or understanding, our souls must in contrition, brokenness from ourselves and our power or efforts, yield to God's Spirit, the Spirit of holiness, to reveal God as the Holy One. And as we begin to know Him in His infinite righteousness, in His burning zeal against all that is sin, and His infinite self-sacrificing love to free the sinner from his sin and to bring him to His own perfection, we shall learn to wonder at and worship this glorious God, to know and deplore our terrible unlikeness to Him, to long and cry for some share in the divine beauty and blessedness of this holiness.

And then will come with new meaning the command "Be holy, as I am holy." You who profess to obey the commands of your God, give this all-surpassing and all-including command the first place in your heart and life that it claims. Be holy in the likeness of God's holiness. Be holy as He is holy. Perhaps the more you meditate and study, the less you can grasp this infinite holiness. Perhaps the more you at times grasp it the more you despair of holiness so divine. Then remember that such breaking down and such despair is just what the command was meant to work. Learn to cease from your own wisdom as well as your own goodness. Draw near in poverty of spirit to let the Holy One show you how utterly above human knowledge or human power is the holiness He demands. To the soul that ceases from self and has no confidence in the flesh He will show and give the holiness to which He calls us.

To such the great gift of holiness in Christ becomes intelligible and acceptable. Christ brings the holiness of God closer by showing it in human conduct and relationships. He brings it within reach by removing the barrier between it and us, between God and us. He brings it closer because He makes us one with himself. "Holy in Christ": our holiness is bestowed by God, held for us, communicated to us, worked mightily in us because we are in *Christ*. That wonderful *in Christ* shows our very life rooted in the life of Christ. That holy Son and Servant of the Father, beautiful in His life of love and obedience on earth, sanctifying himself for us—that life is the ground in which I am planted and rooted, the soil from which I draw as my nourishment its every quality and its very nature. How that word sheds its light both on the revelation "I am holy" and on the command "Be holy, as I am holy" and binds them into one! In Christ I see what God's holiness is and what mine is. In Him both are one and both are mine: in Him I am holy. Abiding and growing up in Him, I can be holy in all manner of living, just as God is holy.

O Most Holy God, we ask you to reveal to your children what it means that you have not only called us to holiness but also called us by this name, "holy ones in Christ Jesus." Oh, that every child of yours might know that he bears this name, that he might know what it means, and know what power there is in it to change him to fit the name. Holy Lord God! Oh, that the time of your visitation might come soon and that each child of yours on earth be known as a holy one!

To this end we pray that you reveal to your saints what your holiness is. Teach us to worship and to wait until you have spoken to our souls with divine power your word "I am holy." May it search out and convict us of our own lack of holiness!

Reveal to us, we pray, that just as you are holy and like a consuming fire, so also is your command in its determined and uncompromising purpose to make us holy. Oh God, let your voice sound through the depths of our being with a power from which there is no escape.

So let us, between your infinite holiness on the one hand and our lack of holiness on the other, be driven and be drawn to accept Christ as our sanctification, to abide in Him as our life and our power to be what you would have us be: "holy in Christ Jesus."

Father, let your Spirit make this precious word life and truth within us. Amen.

Personal Application

1. You are entering anew on the study of a divine mystery. "Lean not on your own understanding" (Proverbs 3:5); wait for the teaching of the Spirit of truth.
2. *In Christ.* A commentator says, "The phrase denotes two moral

facts: first, the act of faith whereby a person lays hold of Christ; and second, the community of life with Him contracted by means of this faith." There is still another fact, the greatest of all: It is by an act of divine power that I am in Christ and am kept in Him. It is this I want to realize: the divineness of my position in Jesus.

3. Grasp the two sides of the truth. You are holy in Christ with a divine holiness. In the faith of that, you are to be holy, to become holy with a human holiness, the divine holiness manifested in all the conduct of a human life.

4. This Christ is a living person, a loving Savior: how He will delight to take complete possession and do all the work in you! Hold on to this as we progress in our study: You have a claim on Christ, on His love and power, to make you holy. As His redeemed one, you are at this moment, whatever and wherever you are, in Him. His holy presence and love are around you. You are in Him, in the enclosure of that tender love that ever encircles you with His holy presence. In that presence, accepted and fulfilled, is your holiness.

Chapter 3

Holiness and Creation

*And God blessed the seventh day and made it holy, because on it
he rested from all the work of creating that he had done.*

Genesis 2:3

In Genesis we have the book of beginnings. To its first three chapters
we are especially indebted for the divine light cast on the many
questions to which human wisdom has not found an answer. In our
search after holiness, we are led here as well. In the whole book of
Genesis the word *holy* occurs only once. But that one time is in such
a connection as to open to us the secret spring from which flows all
that the Bible has to teach or to give us of this heavenly blessing.
The full meaning of the precious word we want to master, of the
priceless blessing we want to take possession of—"sanctified in
Christ"—begins here in what is written of that wondrous act of God
by which He closed His creation work and revealed how wonderfully it would be continued and perfected. When God blessed the
seventh day and sanctified it, He lifted it above the other days and
set it apart to a work and a revelation of himself excelling in glory
all that preceded it. In this simple expression, Scripture reveals to us
the character of God as the Holy One, who makes holy; the way in
which He makes holy, by entering in and resting; and the power of

blessing with which God's making us holy is always accompanied. These three lessons are of deepest importance, containing the root principles of all the Scriptures will teach us in our pursuit of holiness.

1. *God sanctified the Sabbath day.* During the previous six days, from the first calling into existence of heaven and earth down to the making of man, the key word was *God created.* All at once a new word and a new work of God is introduced: *God sanctified.* Something higher than creation, that for which creation is to exist, is now to be revealed; God Almighty is now to be known as God Most Holy. Just as the work of creation shows His power without that power being mentioned, so His making holy the seventh day reveals His character as the Holy One. As omnipotence is the chief of His natural attributes, so holiness is the first of His moral attributes. And just as He alone is Creator, so He alone is Sanctifier; to make holy is His work as truly and exclusively as to create. Blessed is the child of God who truly and fully believes this!

God sanctified the Sabbath day. The word can teach us the nature of the work God does when He makes something holy. Sanctification in heaven cannot be essentially different from sanctification in redemption. God had pronounced all His works, and man the chief of them, very good. And yet they were not holy. The six days' work had nothing of defilement or sin, but still it was not holy. The seventh day especially needed to be made holy for the great work of making man—who was already very good—holy. In Exodus, God says distinctly that He sanctified the Sabbath day with a view to man's sanctification: "So you may know that I am the Lord, who makes you holy" (Exodus 31:13).

Goodness, innocence, purity, and freedom from sin are not holiness. Goodness is the work of omnipotence, an attribute of nature as God created it. Holiness is something infinitely higher. We speak of the holiness of God as His infinite moral perfection; man's moral perfection could only come in the use of his will, freely consenting to and abiding in the will of God. Only in this way could he become holy (if indeed, it were entirely up to him). The seventh day was made holy by God as a pledge that He would make man holy. In the ages that preceded the seventh day, the creation period, God's power, wisdom, and goodness had been displayed. The age to come, in the seventh-day period, is to be the dispensation of holiness. God made holy the seventh day.

2. *God sanctified the Sabbath day, because in it He rested from all His work.* This rest was something real. In creation, God had, as it were, gone out of himself to bring forth something new. In resting He now returns from His creating work into himself to rejoice in His love over the man He has created, and communicates himself to him. This opens up to us the way in which God makes us holy. The connection between the resting and making holy was no arbitrary one. The making holy was no afterthought; in the very nature of things it could not be otherwise. He sanctified because He rested in it. He sanctified *by* resting. As He regards His finished work, especially man, He rejoices in it, and, as we have it in Exodus, "is refreshed." This time of His divine rest is the time in which He will carry on to perfection what He has begun. He will make man, created in His image, in very deed partaker of His highest glory, His holiness.

Where God rests in complacency and love, He makes holy. The presence of God revealing itself, entering in, and taking possession is what constitutes true holiness. As we go down the ages, studying the progressive unfolding of what holiness is, this truth will continually confront us. In God's indwelling in heaven, in His temple on earth, in His beloved Son, in the person of the believer through the Holy Spirit, everywhere we shall find that holiness is not something that man is or does, but that it always comes where God comes. In the deepest meaning of the words: where God enters to rest, there

He sanctifies. When we study the New Testament revelation of the way in which we are to be holy, we shall find this to be one of our earliest and deepest lessons. As we enter into the rest of God we become partakers of His holiness. "We who have believed enter that rest" (Hebrews 4:3); "for anyone who enters God's rest also rests from his own work, just as God did from his" (Hebrews 4:10).

As the soul ceases from its own efforts and rests in Him who has finished all for us, and will finish all in us, and as the soul yields itself in the quiet confidence of true faith to rest in God, it will know what true holiness is. Where the soul enters into the Sabbath stillness of perfect trust, God comes to keep His Sabbath holy, and the soul where He rests He sanctifies. Whether we speak of His own day—"He sanctified it"—or His own people—"sanctified in Christ"—the secret of holiness is always the same: "He sanctified because he rested."

3. *"And God blessed the seventh day and made it holy"* (Genesis 2:3). As used in the first chapter and throughout the book of Genesis, the expression "God blessed" is one of great significance. "Be fruitful and multiply" was to Adam, and later to Noah and Abraham, the divine exposition of its meaning. The blessing with which God blessed Adam and Noah and Abraham was that of fruitfulness and increase, the power to reproduce and multiply. When God blessed the seventh day, He so filled it with the living power of His holiness that in it that holiness might increase and reproduce itself in those who, like Him, seek to enter into its rest and sanctify it. The seventh day is that in which we are now living.

Of each of the creation days it is written, up to the last, "There was evening, and there was morning—" Of the seventh the record has not yet been made; we are living in it now, God's own day of rest and holiness and blessing. Entering into it in a very special manner, and taking possession of it as the time for His rejoicing in His creatures, and manifesting the fullness of His love in sanctifying man, God has made the dispensation in which we now live one of divine and mighty blessing. At the same time He has taught us what the blessing is. Holiness is blessedness. Fellowship with God in His holy rest is blessedness. And as all God's blessings in Christ have but one fountain, God's holiness, so they all have but one aim: to make us partakers of that holiness. God created and blessed with the creation blessing. God sanctified and blessed with the Sabbath the blessing of rest in God and holiness in fellowship with Him.

God's finished work of creation was marred by sin, and our fellowship with Him in the blessing of His holy rest was cut off. The finished work of redemption opened for us a truer rest and a surer entrance into the holiness of God. As He rested in His holy day, so He now rests in His holy Son. In Him we now can enter fully into the rest of God. "Made holy in Christ," let us rest in Him. Let us rest because we see that just as wonderfully as God by His mighty power finished His work of creation, so will He complete and perfect His work of sanctification. Let us yield ourselves to God in Christ, to rest where He rested, to be made holy with His own holiness, and to be blessed with God's own blessing. God the sanctifier is the name now inscribed upon the throne of God the Creator. At the threshold of the history of the human race, there shines this word of infinite promise and hope: "God blessed and sanctified the seventh day because in it he rested."

Blessed Lord God, I bow before you in humble worship. I adore you as God the Creator and God the Sanctifier. You have revealed yourself as God Almighty and God Most Holy. I beseech you to teach me to know and to trust you as such.

I humbly ask you for grace to learn and hold fast the deep spiritual truths you have revealed in making holy the Sabbath day. Your purpose in man's creation is to show forth your holiness and to make him a partaker of it. Oh, teach me to believe in you as God my Creator and

Sanctifier, to believe with my whole heart that the same almighty power that gave the sixth-day blessing of creation, secures to us the seventh-day blessing of sanctification. Your will is our sanctification.

Teach me, Lord, to understand better how this blessing comes. It is where you enter into rest, to refresh and reveal yourself, that you make that place holy. O my God, may my heart be your resting place! In the stillness and confidence of a restful faith, I would rest in you, believing that you do all in me. Let such fellowship with you, and your love and your will be to me the secret of a life of holiness. I ask it in the name of our Lord Jesus, in whom you have sanctified us. Amen.

Personal Application

1. God the Creator is God the Sanctifier. The Omnipotence that did the first work does the second too. I can trust God Almighty to make me holy. God is holy: if God is everything to me, His presence will be my holiness.

2. Rest is ceasing from work, not to work anymore, but to begin a new work. God rests and begins at once to make holy that in which He rests. He created by the word of His power; He rests in His love. Creation was the building of the temple; sanctification is the entering in and taking possession. Oh, that wonderful entering into human nature!

3. God rests only in what is restful, wholly at His disposal. It is in the restfulness of faith that we must look to God the Sanctifier; He will come in and keep His holy Sabbath in the restful soul. We rest in God's rest; God rests in our rest.

4. The God that rests in man whom He made, and in resting sanctifies, and in sanctifying blesses: this is our God. Praise and worship Him, and trust Him to do His work.

5. *Rest!* What a simple word. The rest of God! What an inconceivable *fullness* of life and love. Let us meditate on it and worship Him until it overshadows us and we enter into it—the rest of God. Rest *belongs to* God: He alone can give it by making us share His own.

Chapter 4

Holiness and Revelation

When the Lord saw that he had gone over to look, God called to him from within the bush, "Moses! Moses!" And Moses said, "Here I am." "Do not come any closer," God said. "Take off your sandals, for the place where you are standing is holy ground." . . . At this, Moses hid his face, because he was afraid to look at God.

Exodus 3:4–6

Why was it holy ground? Because God had come there and occupied it. Where God is, there is holiness. It is the presence of God that makes holy. This is the truth we saw in the Garden when man was created; here, where Scripture uses the word *holy* for the second time, it is repeated and enforced. A careful study of the word in the light of the burning bush will further open its deep significance. Let us see what the sacred history, the revelation of God, and Moses teach us about this holy ground.

1. *Note the place this first direct revelation of God to man as the Holy One takes in sacred history.* In the beginning we found the word *holy* used of the seventh day. We found in God's sanctifying the day of rest a promise of a new dispensation—the revelation of the Almighty Creator to be followed by that of the Holy One making holy. But throughout the book of Genesis the word never occurs again; it

is as if God's holiness is in abeyance. Only in Exodus, with the calling of Moses, does it appear again. This is a fact of deep importance. Just as a parent or teacher seeks in early childhood to impress one lesson at a time, so God deals in the education of the human race.

After having in the flood exhibited His righteous judgment against sin, He calls Abraham to be the father of a chosen people. And as the foundation of all God's dealings with that people, He teaches Abraham and his seed, first of all, the lesson of childlike trust—trust in Him as the Almighty, with whom nothing is impossible, and trust in Him as the Faithful One, whose oath cannot be broken. With the growth of Israel to a people we see the revelation advancing to a new stage. The simplicity of childhood gives way to the waywardness of youth, and God must now interfere with the discipline and restriction of the law. Having gained a right to a place in their confidence as the God of their fathers, He prepares them for a further revelation. Of the God of Abraham, the chief attribute is that He is the Almighty One; of the God of Israel, Jehovah, that He is the Holy One.

What is to be the special mark of the new period that is now about to be inaugurated, and which is introduced by the word *holy*?

God tells Moses that He is now about to reveal himself in a new character. He had been known to Abraham as God, the Almighty, the God of promise (Exodus 6:3). He would now manifest himself as Jehovah, the God of fulfillment, especially in the redemption and deliverance of His people from the oppression He had foretold to Abraham. God Almighty is the God of creation. Abraham believed in God "who gives life to the dead and calls things that are not as though they were" (Romans 4:17). Jehovah is the God of redemption and of holiness. With Abraham there was not a word of sin or guilt, and consequently none of redemption or holiness. To Israel the law is to be given to convince of sin and prepare the way for holiness. It is Jehovah, the Holy One of Israel, the Redeemer, who now appears. And it is the presence of this Holy One that makes the ground holy.

2. *And how does this Presence reveal itself?* In the burning bush God makes himself known as dwelling in the midst of the fire. Elsewhere in Scripture the connection between fire and the holiness of God is clearly expressed: "The Light of Israel will become a fire, their Holy One a flame" (Isaiah 10:17). The nature of fire may be either beneficial or destructive. The sun, for instance, may give life and fruitfulness or it may scorch to death. All depends upon occupying the right position, upon where we stand in relation to it. And so wherever God the Holy One reveals himself, we shall find the two sides together: God's holiness as judgment against sin, destroying the sinner who remains in it, and as mercy freeing His people from it. Judgment and mercy always go together. Of the elements of nature, there is none of such spiritual and mighty energy as fire. What it consumes it changes into its own spiritual nature, rejecting as smoke and ashes what cannot be assimilated. And so the holiness of God is that infinite perfection by which He keeps himself free from all that is not divine, and yet has fellowship with the creature and takes him up into union with himself, destroying and casting out all that will not yield to Him.

It is thus as One who dwells in the fire, who is a fire, that God reveals himself at the opening of this new redemption period. With Abraham and the patriarchs, as we have said, there had been little teaching about sin or redemption; the nearness and friendship of God had been revealed. Now the law will be given, sin will be made manifest, the distance from God will be felt in order that man, in learning to know himself and his sinfulness, may learn to know and long for God to make him holy. In all God's revelation of himself, we shall find the combination of the two elements—the one repelling, the other attracting. In His house He will dwell in the midst of Israel, and yet it will be in the awful unapproachable solitude and darkness of the holiest of all within the veil. He will come near to them and yet keep them at a distance. As we study the holiness of God, we shall see in increasing clearness how, like fire, it repels and attracts, how it combines into one His infinite distance and His infinite nearness.

3. *But the distance will be that which comes out first and most strongly.* This we see in Moses. He hid his face, for He feared to look upon God. The first impression that God's holiness produces is that of fear and awe. Until man, both as a creature and a sinner, learns how high God is above him, how different and distant he is from God, the holiness of God will have little real value or attraction. Moses' hiding his face shows us the effect of the drawing near of the Holy One, and the path to His further revelation.

How distinctly this comes out in God's own words: "Do not come any closer. . . . Take off your sandals" (Exodus 3:5). Yes, God had drawn nigh, but Moses may not. God comes near; man must stand back. In the same breath God says, "Draw nigh and draw not nigh." There can be no knowledge of God or nearness to Him where we have not first heard His "draw not nigh." The sense of sin, of unfitness for God's presence, is the groundwork of true knowledge or worship of Him as the Holy One. "Take off your shoes." Shoes are the means of contact with the world, the aids through which the flesh or nature does its will, moves about and does its work. In standing upon holy ground, all this must be put away. It is with naked feet, naked and stripped of every covering, that man must bow before a holy God. Our utter unfitness to draw nigh or have any dealings with the Holy One is the very first lesson we have to learn if we are ever to participate in His holiness. "Putting off" must exercise its condemning power through our whole being, until we come to realize the full extent of its meaning in the great "Put off your old self . . . put on the new self, created to be like God" (Ephesians 4:22, 24), and what "putting off of the sinful nature . . . with the circumcision done by Christ" (Colossians 2:11) is. Yes, all that is of nature and the flesh, all that is of our own doing or willing or working—our very life—must be put off and given over to death, if God as the Holy One is to make himself known to us.

We have seen before that holiness is more than goodness or freedom from sin; even unfallen nature is not holy. Holiness is that awesome glory by which divinity is separated from all that is created. Therefore, even the seraphs veil their faces with their wings when they sing "Holy, holy, holy." But when the distance and the difference is not that of the creature only but of the sinner, who can express, who can realize, the humiliation, the fear, the shame with which we ought to bow before the voice of the Holy One?

This is surely one of the most terrible effects of sin—that it blinds us. We do not know how unholy, how abominable, sin and the sinful nature are in God's sight. We have lost the power to recognize the holiness of God. In heathen philosophy there is no idea of the word *holiness* as expressive of the moral character of its gods. In losing the light of the glory of God, we have lost the power of knowing what sin is.

So God's first work in drawing nigh to us is to make us feel that we may not draw near as we are, that there will have to be a very real and very solemn stripping—and even giving up to death—of all that appears lawful and needful. Not only are our shoes soiled by their contact with this unholy earth, but even our face must be covered and our eyes closed, as a token that the eyes of our heart—all our human wisdom and understanding—are incapable of beholding the Holy One. The first lesson in the school of personal holiness is to fear and to hide our face before the holiness of God. "For this is what the high and lofty One says—he who lives forever, whose name is holy: 'I live in a high and holy place, but also with him who is contrite and lowly in spirit' " (Isaiah 57:15). Contrition, brokenness of spirit, fear and trembling are God's first demand from those who would see His holiness.

Moses was to be the first preacher of the holiness of God. God's first revelation to Moses was the type and pledge of the full communication of His holiness to us in Christ. From Moses' lips the people of Israel, and later from his pen the church of Christ, were to receive the message "Be holy, for I am holy." His preparation for being the messenger of the Holy One was here, where he hid his face because he was afraid to look upon God. It is with our face in the dust; it is in the putting off not only of our shoes but also of all that has been in contact with the world and self and sin that the soul draws nigh to the fire in which God dwells, and that burns but does not consume. Oh, that every believer who seeks to witness for God might learn how the fulfillment of the type of the burning bush is the crucified Christ, and how, as we die with Him, we receive that baptism of fire. Only so can we learn what it is to be holy as He is holy.

Most Holy God, I have seen you who dwell in the fire. I have heard your voice, "Draw not nigh; take off your shoes." And my soul has feared to look upon God, the Holy One. And yet, O God, I must see you! You created me to bear your likeness. You taught that this likeness is your holiness: "Be holy, as I am holy." But how shall I know how to be holy unless I see you? To be holy I must look upon God.

I bless you for the revelation of yourself in the burning bush and in the fire of the accursed tree. I bow in amazement and deep abasement at the great sight: your Son in the weakness of His human nature, in the fire, burning but not consumed. O my God, in fear and trembling I have yielded myself as a sinner to die like Him. Oh, let the fire consume all that is unholy in me! Let me, too, know you as the God that dwells in the fire, to melt down and purge out and destroy what is not of you, to save and take up into your own holiness that which is your own. I bow in the dust before this great mystery. Reveal to me your holiness that I too may be its witness and its messenger on earth. Amen.

Personal Application

1. Holiness is the fire of God. Praise God that there is a power that can consume the vile and the dross, a power that will not leave it undisturbed. "The bush was on fire but it did not burn up" (Exodus 3:2) is not only the motto of the church in time of persecution, it is the watchword of every soul in God's sanctifying work.

2. There is a new theology that only speaks of the love of God as seen in the cross. It does not see the glory of His righteousness or His righteous judgment. This is not the God of Scripture. "Our God is a consuming fire" (Hebrews 12:29) is New Testament theology. To "worship God acceptably with reverence and awe" (Hebrews 12:28) is New Testament Christianity. In holiness, judgment and mercy meet.

3. Holiness is the fear of God. Hiding the face before God for fear, not daring to look or speak—this is the beginning of rest in God. It is not yet the true rest, but on the way to it. May God give us a deep fear of whatever could grieve or anger Him. May we have a deep fear of ourselves and of all that is of the old, condemned nature, lest it rise again. "The spirit of the fear of the Lord" is the first manifestation of the spirit of holiness, and prepares the way for the joy of holiness. "Walking in the fear of the Lord, and in the comfort of the Holy Ghost"; these are the two sides of the Christian life.

4. The holiness of God was revealed to Moses that he might be its messenger. The church needs nothing so much today as men and women who can testify for the holiness of God. Will you be one of those?

Additional Note

The connection between the fear of God and holiness is intimate. There are some who seek earnestly for holiness and yet never exhibit it in a light that will attract the world, or even believers, because this element is lacking. It is the fear of the Lord that works meekness and gentleness in us, that deliverance from self-confidence and self-consciousness that forms the true groundwork of a godly character. The passages of God's Word in which the two words are linked together are well worth careful study.

Who is like unto you,
glorious in holiness,
fearful in praises?
In your fear will I worship
toward your holy temple.
O fear the Lord, you his holy ones.
O worship the Lord in
the beauty of holiness.
Fear before him, all the earth.
Let them praise your great
and terrible name;
holy is he.
The fear of the Lord is
the beginning of wisdom;
and the knowledge of the Holy One
is understanding.
The Lord of hosts,
him shall you sanctify;
let him be your fear,
and let him be your dread.
Perfecting holiness in
the fear of the Lord.
Like as he which called you is holy,
be yourselves also holy;

and if you call on him as father,
pass the time of your sojourning in fear.

This is but a sampling of Scriptures that speak of fear and holiness together. And so on through the whole of Scripture, from the Song of Moses to the Song of the Lamb: "Who shall not fear you, O Lord! and glorify your name, for you only are holy." If we meditate on these passages and yield to their message, we will become sensitive and fearful of offending God in any way. We will especially fear to enter His holy presence with what is human and carnal, with anything of our own wisdom and effort. With deep conviction we will recognize that this fear of God is the very essence of the holiness we are to follow after.

This fear of God will make us, like Moses, fall down and hide our face before God's presence and wait for His own Holy Spirit to open our eyes and breathe in us the worship with which to draw nigh to Him. This holy fear works in us that stillness of soul that leads it to rest in God and opens the way for the secret of holiness: God keeping His Sabbath and sanctifying the soul in which He rests.

Holiness and Redemption

Consecrate to me every firstborn male.

Exodus 13:2

All the firstborn are mine. When I struck down all the firstborn in Egypt, I set apart for myself every firstborn in Israel. . . . They are to be mine. I am the Lord.

Numbers 3:13

I am the Lord who brought you up out of Egypt to be your God; therefore be holy, because I am holy.

Leviticus 11:45

I have redeemed you . . . you are mine.

Isaiah 43:1

At Horeb the first mention of the word *holy* in the history of fallen man was connected with the inauguration of a new period in the revelation of God, that of redemption. In the Passover we have the first manifestation of what redemption is, and here the more frequent use of the word *holy* begins. In the feast of unleavened bread we have the symbol of putting off the old and putting on the new, to which redemption through the blood leads. Of the seven days we read, "On the first day hold a sacred assembly, and another one on the seventh day" (Exodus 12:16). The meeting of the redeemed people to commemorate their deliverance was a holy gathering; they met under the covering of their Redeemer, the Holy One. As soon as the people had been redeemed from Egypt, God's very first word to them was "Consecrate to me every firstborn male. The first offspring . . . belongs to me" (see Exodus 13:2). The Word reveals how ownership is one of the central thoughts both in redemption and in sanctification, the link that binds them together. And though the word here speaks only of the firstborn, they are a type of the whole people.

We know how all growth and organization commence from a center, around which in ever-widening circles the life of the organism spreads. If holiness in the human race is to be true and real, as coming from God, it must be the result of a self-appropriation. And so the firstborn are sanctified, and afterward the priests in their place, as the type of what the whole people are to be as God's firstborn among the nations, His peculiar treasure, "a holy nation." This idea of ownership as related to redemption and sanctification comes out with special clearness when God speaks of the exchange of the priests for the firstborn (Numbers 3:12–13; 8:16–17): "They [the Levites] are the Israelites who are to be given wholly to me. . . . I have taken them as my own in place of the firstborn, the first male offspring from every Israelite woman. Every firstborn male in Israel . . . is mine. When I struck down all the firstborn in Egypt, I set them apart for myself."

Let us try to understand the relationship that exists between redemption and holiness. At Creation God sanctified the seventh day by taking possession of it. He blessed it, He rested in it, and He refreshed himself. Where God enters and rests, there is holiness. The more perfectly the object is fitted for Him to enter and dwell, the more perfect the holiness. The seventh day was sanctified as the period for man's sanctification. The very first step God took to lead man to His holiness was the command not to eat of the tree. Man disobeyed this command and fell, experiencing spiritual death. God did not give up His plan, but now had to pursue a different and slower path.

After centuries of needed preparation, He revealed himself as the Redeemer. The people whom He had chosen and formed for himself, He gave up to oppression and slavery that their hearts might be prepared to long for and welcome a deliverer. In a series of mighty wonders He proved himself the conqueror of their enemies, and then in the blood of the Passover Lamb on their doors, He taught them what redemption is, not only from an unjust oppressor here on earth but also from the righteous judgment their sins deserved. The Passover was to be to them the transition from the seen and temporal to the unseen and spiritual, revealing God not only as the Mighty but also as the Holy One, freeing them not only from the house of bondage but also from the destroying angel.

Having thus redeemed them, He told them they were His own. During their stay at Sinai and in the wilderness, the thought was continually pressed upon them that they were the Lord's people, whom He had made His own by the strength of His arm that He might make them holy for himself, even as He is holy. The purpose of redemption is possession, and the purpose of possession is likeness to Him who is Redeemer and Owner. That likeness is holiness.

The sanctifying of the firstborn teaches us more than one lesson with regard to holiness and the way it is attained as a result of redemption.

First of all, we must understand how inseparable redemption and holiness are. Neither can exist without the other. Only redemption leads to holiness. If I am seeking holiness, I must abide in the clear and full experience of being redeemed, and as such of being owned and possessed by God. Redemption is too often looked at from its negative side of deliverance *from* sin. Its real glory is the positive element of being redeemed *unto* God. Full possession of a house means occupation. If I own a house without occupying it, it can become the home of decay and corruption. God has redeemed me and made me His own with the view of gaining complete possession of me. He says of my soul, "It is mine," and seeks to have His right of ownership acknowledged and made fully manifest. That will be perfect holiness, where God has entered in and taken complete and entire possession. It is redemption that gives God His right and power over me. Redemption sets me free for God to possess and bless. It is redemption realized and filling my soul that will bring assurance and the experience of all that His power can work in me. In God, redemption and sanctification are one. The more redemption as a divine reality takes control of me, the closer I will be linked to the Redeemer.

Only holiness brings the assurance and enjoyment of redemption. If I am seeking to hold on to redemption at a lower level, I may be deceived. If I have become unwatchful or careless, I should be wary of the idea of trusting in redemption apart from holiness. To Israel God spoke, "I brought you up out of the land of Egypt: therefore you shall be holy, for I am holy." It is God the Redeemer who made us His own, who calls us also to be holy. Let holiness be the most essential, the most precious part of redemption: the yielding of ourselves to Him who has taken us as His own.

A second lesson implied is the connection between God's work and man's work in sanctification. To Moses the Lord said, "Sanctify unto me all the firstborn." And afterward he said, "I sanctified all the firstborn for myself." What God does is to be carried out and appropriated through us. When He tells us that we are made holy in Christ Jesus, that we are His holy ones, He speaks not only of His purpose but also of what He has actually done; we have been sanctified in the one offering of Christ and by our being created anew in Him. But this work has a human side. To us is given the call to be holy, to follow after holiness, to perfect holiness. God has made us His own, and allows us to say that we are His, but He waits for us to yield to Him an enlarged entrance into the secret place of our inner being so that He can fill us with His fullness. Holiness is not something we bring to God or do for Him. Holiness is what there is of God in us. God has made us His own in redemption that He might make himself our own in sanctification. Our work in becoming holy is the bringing our whole life, every part of it, into subjection to the rule of our holy God, putting every member and every power upon His altar.

This answers the question about the sudden and the gradual aspects of sanctification, between its being a thing once-for-all complete and yet imperfect and needing to be perfected. What God sanctifies is holy with a divine and perfect holiness as His gift. Man has to sanctify himself by acknowledging this and then maintaining and carrying out that holiness in relation to all his life before God and man. God sanctified the Sabbath day. Man has to sanctify it by keeping it holy. God sanctified the firstborn as His own; Israel had to sanctify them by giving them over to God. God is holy. We are to sanctify Him by acknowledging and adoring and honoring that holiness. God has sanctified His great name; His name is Holy. We sanctify or hallow that name as we fear and trust and use it as the revelation of His holiness. God sanctified Christ. Christ sanctified himself, manifesting in His personal will and action perfect conformity to the holiness of the Father. God has sanctified us in Christ Jesus. We are to be holy by yielding ourselves to the power of that holiness, by acting it out in our daily life and walk. The objective divine gift that was bestowed once for all and completely must be appropriated as a subjective personal possession; we must cleanse ourselves, perfecting holiness. Redeemed unto holiness; just as the two thoughts are linked in the mind and work of God, they must be linked in our heart and life.

When Isaiah announced the second, the true redemption, it was given to him even more clearly and fully than to Moses to reveal the name of God as "Your Redeemer, the Holy One of Israel" (Isaiah 48:17). The more we study this name and hallow it, and worship God by it, the more inseparably will the words *holiness* and *redemption* become connected, and we shall see that just as the Redeemer is the Holy One, the redeemed are holy too. Isaiah says of "the Way of Holiness," the "redeemed will walk there" (Isaiah 35:8–9). The redemption that comes forth from the holiness of God must lead into holiness as well. We must understand that to be redeemed in Christ is to be holy in Christ. Then the call of our redeeming God will acquire new meaning: "I am holy: be holy."

O Lord God, the Holy One of Israel and her Redeemer, I worship before you in deep humility. I confess with shame that I long followed you more as the Redeemer than as the Holy One. I had yet to learn that it was as the Holy One that you redeemed us, that redemption was the outcome and the fruit of your holiness. I only thought of being redeemed from bondage and death: like Israel, I did not understand that without fellowship and conformity to yourself, redemption loses its value.

Most holy God! I praise you for the patience with which you bear with the selfishness and the slowness of your redeemed ones. I praise you for the teaching of the Spirit of your holiness that leads your saints to see how it is your holiness and the call to become partaker of it that gives redemption its value. With love and joy and thanksgiving that cannot be expressed, I praise you for Christ Jesus, who has been made unto me sanctification and redemption! O God, in speechless adoration I fall down to worship the Love that passes knowledge, the Love that has accomplished redemption for us, and I believe that as we come before you, holy in Christ, you will fulfill all your glorious purposes in us according to your great power. Amen.

Personal Application

1. "Redemption through his blood." This blood stands at the threshold of the pathway of holiness. It is the blood of the sacrifice that the fire of God consumed and yet could not consume. That blood has such power of holiness in it that we read we are "sanctified by his blood." Always think of holiness, or pray for it, as one redeemed by the blood. Live under the covering of the blood in its daily cleansing power.

2. It is only as we know the holiness of God as fire, and bow before His righteous judgment, that we can appreciate the preciousness of the blood or the reality of redemption. As long as we only think of the love of God as goodness, we may aim at being good; faith in God who redeems will awaken in us the need and the joy of being holy in Christ.

3. Have you understood the right of ownership God has in what He has redeemed? Have you heard Him say to you, "You are mine"? Very humbly ask God to say it to you. Listen for His response.

4. The holiness of the creature has its origin in the divine will, in the divine election, redemption, and possession. Give yourself over to this will of God and rejoice in it.

5. As God created, so He redeemed, to sanctify. Have great faith in Him for this.

6. Let God have entire possession of you, and this means you will be at His disposal. Holiness is His; our holiness is to allow Him, the Holy One, to be all.

Chapter 6

Holiness and Glory

Who among the gods is like you, O Lord? Who is like you—
majestic in holiness, awesome in glory, working wonders?
In your unfailing love you will lead the people you have
redeemed. In your strength you will guide
them to your holy dwelling . . . [the holy place],
O Lord, your hands established.

Exodus 15:11, 13, 17

These words advance us another step in the revelation of holiness. We have here for the first time holiness predicated of God himself. He is glorious in holiness, and it is to the dwelling place of His holiness that He is guiding His people.

Let us first note the expression used here: "majestic in holiness." Throughout Scripture we find the majesty or glory and the holiness of God mentioned together. In Exodus 29:43 we read, "The place will be consecrated by my glory," that glory of the Lord of which we later read that it filled the house. The glory of an object, of a thing or person, is its intrinsic worth or excellence; to glorify is to remove everything that could hinder the full revelation of that excellence. In the holiness of God His glory is hidden; in the glory of God His holiness is manifested. His glory, the revelation of himself as the

Holy One, would make the house holy. In the same way the two are connected in Leviticus 10:3: "Among those who approach me I will show myself holy; in the sight of all the people I will be honored." The acknowledgment of His holiness in the priests would be the manifestation of His glory to the people. So, too, in the song of the seraphim (Isaiah 6:3): "Holy, holy, holy is the Lord Almighty; the whole earth is full of his glory." God is He who dwells in a light that is unapproachable, whom no man has seen or can see. It is the light of the knowledge of the glory of God that He places in our hearts. The glory is that which can be seen and known of the invisible and unapproachable light; that light itself, and the glorious fire of which it is the expression, is the holiness of God. Holiness is not so much an attribute of God as the comprehensive summary of all His perfections.

On the shore of the Red Sea Israel praised God: "Who among the gods is like you, O Lord? Who is like you—majestic in holiness?" (Exodus 15:11). He is the Incomparable One; there is none like Him. Where has He proved this and revealed the glory of His holiness?

With Moses in Horeb we saw God's glory in the fire, in its double aspect of salvation and destruction, consuming what could not be purified, purifying what was not consumed. Here, too, in the song of Moses, Israel sings of judgment and of mercy. The pillar of fire and the cloud came between the camp of the Egyptians and the camp of Israel—a cloud and darkness to the Egyptians, but light by night to God's people. The two thoughts run through the whole song. Following the ascription of holiness (Exodus 15:11), we find the destruction of verse 12: "You stretched out your right hand and the earth swallowed them." This is the glory of holiness as judgment and destruction of the Enemy.

"In your unfailing love you will lead the people you have redeemed. In your strength you will guide them to your holy dwelling" (Exodus 15:13). This is the glory of holiness in mercy and redemption—a holiness that not only delivers but also guides to the habitation of holiness, where the Holy One is to dwell with and in His people. So in the inspiration of the hour of triumph, it is revealed that the great object and fruit of redemption, as worked out by the Holy One, is to be His indwelling; with nothing short of this can the Holy One rest content or the full glory of His holiness be made manifest.

Observe further how as in the redemption of His people God's holiness is revealed, so in the song of redemption the personal ascription of holiness to God is found. We know how in Scripture, after some striking special interposition of God as Redeemer, the special influence of the Spirit is manifested in some song of praise. In these outbursts of worship, it is remarkable how God is praised as the Holy One. See it in the song of Hannah: "There is no one holy like the Lord" (1 Samuel 2:2). The language of the seraphim (Isaiah 6) is that of a song of adoration. In the great day of Israel's deliverance the song will be "The Lord is my strength and my song. . . . Sing to the Lord, for he has done glorious things. . . . Shout aloud and sing for joy, people of Zion, for great is the Holy One of Israel among you" (Isaiah 12:2, 5–6). Mary sings, "For the Mighty One has done great things for me—holy is his name" (Luke 1:49). The book of Revelation reveals the living creatures giving glory and honor and thanks to Him that sits on the throne: "Day and night they never stop saying: 'Holy, holy, holy is the Lord God Almighty, who was, and is, and is to come'" (Revelation 4:8). And when the song of Moses and of the Lamb is sung by the sea of glass it will still be "Who will not fear you, O Lord, and bring glory to your name? For you alone are holy" (Revelation 15:4). It is in the moments of highest anointing, under the fullest manifestation of God's redeeming power, that His servants speak of His holiness. In Psalm 97:12 we read, "Rejoice in the Lord, you who are righteous, and praise his holy name." And in Psalm 99 (where its thrice-repeated holy has been called the echo on earth of the Thrice Holy of heaven), we sing:

> Let them praise your great and
>   awesome name—he is holy.
> Exalt the Lord our God
>   and worship at his footstool;
>   he is holy.
> Exalt the Lord our God
>   and worship at his holy mountain,
>   for the Lord our God is holy. (vv. 3, 5, 9)

Only under the influence of high spiritual elevation and joy can God's holiness be fully apprehended or rightly worshiped. The sentiment that becomes us as we worship the Holy One, that fits us for knowing and worshiping Him aright, is the spirit of praise that sings and shouts for joy in the experience of His full salvation.

But does this contradict the lesson we learned at Horeb, when God said, "Do not come any closer. . . . Take off your sandals" (Exodus 3:5), and where Moses feared and hid his face? Is hiding our face not the fitting attitude for us as creatures and sinners? Yes, it is. But the two sentiments are not contradictory; rather they are indispensable to each other. The fear is the preparation for the praise and the glory. Is it not the same Moses who hid his face and feared to look upon God, who afterward beheld His glory until his own face shone with a brightness that men could not bear to look upon? Is not this song that speaks of God as glorious in holiness also the song of Moses who feared and hid his face? Have we not seen in the fire and in God—especially in His holiness—a twofold aspect: consuming and purifying, repelling and attracting, judging and saving? In each case the latter is not only the accompaniment but also the result of the former.

We find that the deeper the humbling and awe in God's holy

presence, the more real and complete is the putting off of self, even to the complete death of the old man and his will. And the more hearty the giving up of what is sinful, the deeper and fuller will be the praise and joy with which we sing the song of redemption: "Who is like you—majestic in holiness, awesome in glory, working wonders?" (Exodus 15:11). The song harmonizes the apparently conflicting elements, for the next verse says, "You stretched out your right hand and the earth swallowed them." Yes, I will sing of judgment *and* of mercy. I will rejoice with trembling as I praise the Holy One. As I look upon the two sides of His holiness, as revealed to the Egyptians and the Israelites, I remember that what was there separated is in me united. By nature I am the Egyptian, an enemy doomed to destruction; by grace, an Israelite chosen for redemption. In me the fire must consume and destroy; only as judgment does its work can mercy fully save. It is only as I tremble before the searching light, the burning fire, and the consuming heat of the Holy One, as I yield my Egyptian nature to be judged, condemned, and slain, that the Israelite will be redeemed to know his God as the God of salvation and to rejoice in Him.

Praise God! The judgment is past. In Christ, the burning bush, the fire of the divine holiness has done its double work. In Him sin was condemned in the flesh, in Him we are free. In giving up His will to death and doing God's will, Christ sanctified himself, and in that will we are sanctified too. His crucifixion with its judgment of the flesh and His death with its entire putting off of what is natural are not only *for* us but are, in fact, *ours*—a life and power working within us by His Spirit. Day by day we abide in Him. With fear and trembling but with rejoicing we take our stand in Him. The power of holiness as judgment against sin and flesh allows it to accomplish its glorious work. We give thanks at the remembrance of His holiness. And so the shout of salvation rings ever deeper, truer, louder throughout life: "Who is like you—majestic in holiness, awesome in glory, working wonders?"

With my whole heart would I join in this song of redemption and rejoice in you as the God of my salvation.

Let your Spirit, from whom these words of holy joy and triumph come, so reveal within me your great redemption as a personal experience, that my whole life may be one song of holy fear and adoring wonder. I especially ask that my whole heart be filled with yourself, glorious in holiness, fearful in praises, who alone does wonders. Let the awe of your holiness reveal all there is of self and flesh. Lead me in my worship to deny and crucify my own wisdom that the Spirit of your holiness may breathe in me. Prepare me to praise you without ceasing at the remembrance of your holiness. As my Redeemer, you make me holy. With my whole heart I trust you to sanctify me wholly. I believe in your promise.

Who is like you? There is none like you. Amen.

Personal Application

1. God is glorified in the holiness of His people. True holiness always gives glory to God alone. Live to the glory of God: that is holiness. Live a holy life: that will glorify God. To lose sight of self and seek only God's glory is holiness.

2. Praise gives glory to God, and is thus an element of holiness. "You are holy, you that inhabit the praises of Israel."

3. God's holiness, His holy redeeming love, is cause for unceasing joy and praise. Praise God every day for it. But you cannot do this unless you live in it. When we understand that whatever we see of God's glory is simply the expression of His holiness, His holiness will become so glorious to us that we cannot help but rejoice in it and in Him.

4. The spirit of the fear of the Lord and the spirit of praise may at

first glance appear to be at variance. But they are not. The humility that fears the Holy One will also praise Him: "You that fear the Lord: praise the Lord." The lower and more humbly we lie in the fear of God and the fear of self, the more surely will He lift us up in due time to praise Him.

Chapter 7

Holiness and Obedience

*You yourselves have seen what I did to Egypt, and how I carried
you on eagles' wings and brought you to myself. Now if you
obey me fully and keep my covenant, then out of all nations
you will be my treasured possession. . . .
You will be for me . . . a holy nation.*

Exodus 19:4–6

Israel has reached Horeb. The law is to be given and the covenant
made. Here are God's first words to the people; He speaks of redemption and its blessing, fellowship with himself: "You yourselves
have seen . . . how I . . . brought you to myself." He speaks of holiness as His purpose in redemption: "You will be for me . . . a holy
nation." As the link between the two He places obedience: "If you
obey me fully and keep my covenant." God's will is the expression
of His holiness; as we do His will, we come into contact with His
holiness. The link between redemption and holiness is obedience.

This takes us back to what we saw at Creation. God sanctified
the seventh day as the time for sanctifying man. And what was the
first thing He did? He gave him a commandment. Obedience to that
commandment would have opened the door. It would have been the
entrance into the holiness of God.

Holiness is a moral attribute; it is that which a free will chooses and determines for itself. What God creates and gives is only naturally good; what man wills to have of God and His will, and truly appropriates, has moral worth and leads to holiness.

At Creation God manifested His wise and good will. He speaks His will through His commands. As that holy will enters man's will and as man accepts it and unites himself with God's will he becomes holy. After Creation, on the seventh day, God enrolled man in His work of sanctification to make him holy. Obedience is the path to holiness because it is the path to union with God's holy will. With man before the Fall as with fallen man, in redemption here and in glory above, in all the angels and even in Christ himself, *obedience* is the path to holiness. Obedience itself is not holiness, but as the will opens itself to accept and to do the will of God, God communicates himself and His holiness. To obey His voice is to follow Him as He leads the way to the full revelation and communication of himself and His blessed nature.

Obedience is not knowledge of the will of God, it is not even approval; it is not the will to do it, but the doing of it. Knowledge and approval and will must all lead to action; the will of God must be done: "If you obey me fully and keep my covenant." Here it is not faith, not worship, not profession that God asks of His people when He speaks of holiness. It is obedience. God's will must be done on earth as in heaven. "You will remember to obey all my commands and will be consecrated to your God" (Numbers 15:40). "Consecrate yourselves and be holy. . . . Keep my decrees and follow them. I am the Lord, who makes you holy" (Leviticus 20:7–8). "Keep my commands and follow them. I am the Lord. . . . I must be acknowledged as holy by the Israelites. I am the Lord, who makes you holy and who brought you out of Egypt to be your God. I am the Lord" (Leviticus 22:31–33).

A moment's reflection makes this clear. A man's work shows

what he is. I may know what is good and yet not agree to it. I may agree but still not will to do it. In a certain sense I may even will a thing but lack the energy or self-sacrifice or power that will motivate me to do it. Thinking is easier than willing, and willing is easier than doing. *Action alone* proves whether the object of my interest has complete mastery over me. God wants His will done. This alone is obedience. Only in this way is it seen whether the whole heart, with all its strength and will, has fully yielded to the will of God; whether we live His will and are ready by any sacrifice to make it our own by doing it. God has no other way of making us holy. "Keep my decrees and follow them. I am the Lord, who makes you holy" (Leviticus 20:8).

To all seekers after holiness this lesson is of deep importance. Obedience is not holiness. Holiness is something far higher, something that comes from God to us—or rather something of God coming into us. But obedience is nonetheless indispensable to holiness. Holiness cannot be had without it. As your heart seeks to follow God's Word and looks back in faith to what God has done in making you holy in Christ, as you look ahead to what God will do through His Holy Spirit to fulfill the promise "The God of peace, sanctify you through and through" (1 Thessalonians 5:23), never for one moment forget to be obedient.

"Now if you obey me fully and keep my covenant . . . you will be for me . . . a holy nation" (Exodus 19:5–6). Begin by doing at once whatever appears right to do. Give up at once whatever conscience tells you is not according to the will of God. Do not only pray for light and strength but act. Do what God says. "Whoever does God's will is my brother" (Mark 3:35), Jesus says. Every son of God has been begotten of the will of God; in doing that will he has his life. To do the Father's will is the meat, the strength, and the mark of every child of God.

Surrender to such a life of simple and entire obedience is

implicit to being a faithful Christian. It is sad that so many Christians, either from lack of correct instruction or from insufficient attention to the teaching of God's Word, have never realized the place of supreme importance that obedience has in the Christian life. They do not know that through obedience alone is found the way to the love, the likeness, and the glory of God. We have all suffered at one time or another from ignorance of that fact. In our prayers and striving for perfect peace and the rest of faith, the abiding joy and increased power of the Holy Spirit, something has hindered the blessing or caused the rapid loss of what had been apprehended. A wrong concept about the absolute necessity of obedience is usually the cause. *The freedom and mighty power of grace, from our conversion onward, moves toward the object of restoring us to active obedience and harmony with God's will, from which we had fallen through the first sin in the Garden.* Obedience leads to God and His holiness. In obedience the will is molded, the character formed, and the inner man is built up, which God can clothe and adorn with the beauty of holiness.

When a Christian discovers that this has been the missing link, the cause of failure and darkness, he must in a grand act of surrender, deliberately choose obedience—universal, wholehearted obedience—as the law of his life in the power of the Holy Spirit. May he make his own the words of Israel at Sinai, in answer to the message of God we are considering: "Everything the Lord has said we will do" (Exodus 24:3); "We will do everything the Lord has said; we will obey" (Exodus 24:7). What the law could not do, in that it was weak through the flesh, God has done by the gift of His Son and His Spirit. The giving of the Law at Sinai on tables of stone has been succeeded by the Spirit's giving of the Law on the table of the heart. The Holy Spirit is the power of obedience. He prepares our hearts to be the dwelling place of the Holy One. In this faith, let us yield ourselves to a life of obedience. It is the New Testament path to the realization of the promise: "Now if you obey me fully and keep my covenant . . . you will be for me . . . a holy nation" (Exodus 19:5–6).

We have already seen how holiness in its very nature assumes the truth of a personal relationship to God, His personal presence. "[I] brought you to myself. Now if you obey . . . you will be for me . . . a holy nation" (Exodus 19:4–6). As we understand and hold fast this personal element, obedience will become possible and will lead to holiness. Mark well God's words: "Now if you obey me fully and keep my covenant, then out of all nations you will be my treasured possession" (Exodus 19:5). The voice is more than a law or a book; it always implies a living person and communication with Him. This is the secret of gospel obedience: hearing the voice and following the lead of Jesus as a personal friend and living Savior. It is being led by the Spirit of God, having Him reveal the presence, the will, and the love of the Father that will work in us that personal relationship that the New Testament refers to when it speaks of doing everything as unto the Lord, pleasing God.

Such obedience is the pathway to holiness. Its every act is a link to the living God, a surrender of the being for God's will, for God himself to take possession. In the process of assimilation, slow but sure, by which the will of God, as the meat of our souls, is accepted into our inmost being, our spiritual nature is strengthened, spiritualized, growing up into a holy temple in which God can reveal himself and take up His abode.

When God sanctified the seventh day as His period of making holy, He taught us that He could not do it all at once. The revelation and communication of holiness must be gradual, as man is prepared to receive it. God's sanctifying work with each of us, as with the race, takes time. The time it needs and seeks is the life of daily, hourly obedience. All that is spent in self-will and not in living relationship to the Lord is lost. But when the heart seeks day by day to hearken to His voice and to obey it, the Holy One himself watches over His words to fulfill them: "You will be for me . . . a holy nation" (Exodus 19:6). In a way of which the soul can have little concept, God will overshadow and make His abode in the obedient heart. The habit of always listening for His voice and obeying it will only be the building of the temple; the living God himself, the Holy One, will come to take up His abode. The glory of the Lord will fill the house and the promise be made true: "The place will be consecrated by my glory" (Exodus 29:43).

"[I] brought you to myself. Now if you obey . . . you will be for me . . . a holy nation" (Exodus 19:4–6). Seekers after holiness: God has brought you to himself. Now His voice speaks to you the thoughts of His heart, so that as you take them in and make them your own, and make His will your own by living and doing it, you may enter into the most complete union with Him, the union of will as well as of life, and so become a holy people unto Him. Let obedience, listening to and doing the will of God, be the joy and the glory of your life. It will give you access unto the holiness of God.

O my God, you have redeemed me for yourself that you might have me wholly as your own, possessing, filling my inmost being with your own likeness, your perfect will, and the glory of your holiness. You seek to train me, in the power of a free and loving will, to take your will and make it my own so that in the very center of my being your perfection may dwell. Help me accept and keep your words, and master their meaning, which reveals your will.

Let me live day by day in such fellowship with you that I may indeed in everything hear your voice, the living voice of the living God, speaking to me. Let the Holy Spirit, the Spirit of your holiness, be to me your voice guiding me in the path of simple, childlike obedience. I bless you that I have seen that Christ, in whom I am holy, was the obedient one, that in obedience He sanctified himself to become my sanctification, and that abiding in Him, I am abiding in your will. I will indeed obey your will: make me one of your holy nation, a peculiar treasure above all people. Amen.

Personal Application

1. "He . . . became obedient to death" (Philippians 2:8). "Although he was a son, he learned obedience from what he suffered" (Hebrews 5:8). "I have come to do your will" (Hebrews 10:9). In this will we are sanctified. Christ's example teaches us that obedience is the only path to the holiness or the glory of God. Let this be your commitment: a surrender in everything to seek and do the will of God.

2. We are "holy in Christ"—in this Christ who did the will of God and was obedient unto death. We are in Him; in Him we are holy. His obedience is the soil in which we are planted and must be rooted. He said, "It is my meat to do his will"; obedience was the sustenance of His life; in doing God's will He drew divine nourishment; it must be so with us too.

3. As you study what it is to abide in Christ, as you rejoice that you are in Him, always remember it is that same Christ who obeyed in whom God has planted you.

4. If ever you feel perplexed about holiness, just yield yourself again to do God's will, and then do it. It is ours to obey, it is God's to sanctify.

5. Christ sanctified himself by obedience, by doing the will of God, and in that will we have been sanctified. For our part, in accepting that will as done by Him and in accepting Him, we are made holy. I am in Him; in every act of living obedience, I enter into living fellowship with Him and draw the power of His life into mine.

6. Obedience depends upon hearing the voice of God. Do not assume you know the will of God. Pray and wait for the inward teaching of the Spirit.

Chapter 8

Holiness and Indwelling

Then have them make a sanctuary [holy place] for me,
and I will dwell among them.

Exodus 25:8

The place will be consecrated by my glory. . . . Then I will
dwell among the Israelites and be their God.

Exodus 29:43, 45

The presence of God makes holy, even when it descends for only a short time, as at Horeb in the burning bush. How much more must that presence make holy the place where it dwells, where it fixes its permanent abode! A vivid example is that the place where God dwells came to be called the holy place, "the holy place where the Most High dwells" (Psalms 46:4). All around where God dwelt was holy: the holy city, the mountain of God's holiness, His holy house, until we come within the veil to the most holy place—the Holy of Holies. It is as the indwelling God that He sanctifies His house, that He reveals himself as the Holy One in Israel, and that He makes us holy too.

Because God is holy, the house in which He dwells is holy. Holiness is the only attribute of God that He can and does communicate to His house. Among men there is a very close link between the character of a house and its occupants. When there is no obstacle to prevent it, the house naturally reflects the master's likeness. Holiness expresses not so much an attribute as the essential being of God in His infinite perfection, and His house testifies to this truth: He is holy, where He dwells He must have holiness, and His indwelling makes a place holy. In His first command to His people to build Him a holy place, God distinctly said that it was so that He might dwell among them; the dwelling in the house was to be the shadow of His dwelling in the midst of His people. The house with its holiness thus leads us on to the holiness of His dwelling among His redeemed ones.

The holy place, the habitation of God's holiness, was the center of all God's work in making Israel holy. Everything connected with it was holy. The altar, the priests, the sacrifices, the oil, the bread, the vessels—all were holy because they belonged to God. From the house there issued the twofold voice: God's call to be holy and God's promise to make holy. God's claim was manifested in the demand for cleansing, for atonement, for holiness, in all who were to draw near, whether as priests or worshipers. And God's promise shone forth from His house in the provision for making holy, in the sanctifying power of the altar, of the blood and the oil. The house embodied the two sides that are united in holiness, the repelling and the attracting, the condemning and the saving. First by keeping the people at a distance, then by inviting and bringing them near, God's house was the great symbol of His own holiness. He had come near to dwell among them; but even then they were not permitted to enter the secret place of His presence.

All these things are written on our behalf. As the Indwelling One God is the sanctifier of His people: the indwelling presence alone makes us holy. This becomes especially clear if we note that the nearer the presence was, the greater the degree of holiness. Because

God dwelt among them, the camp was holy: all uncleanness was to be removed from it. But the holiness of the court of the tabernacle was even greater: uncleanness that might be allowed in the camp would not be tolerated there. The holy place was even holier because it was closer to God. And the inner sanctuary—where the presence dwelt on the mercy seat—was the holiest of all. The principle still holds. Holiness is measured by nearness to God; the more there is of His presence, the more there is of true holiness. Perfect indwelling means perfect holiness. None is holy but the Lord; there is no holiness except in Him. He cannot part with some of His holiness and give it to us apart from himself; we have only as much holiness as we have of God himself. And to have Him truly and fully, we must have Him as the Indwelling One. But even His indwelling in a house or place without life or spirit is only a faint shadow of the true indwelling as the Living One, as when He enters into our very being and fills us with His own life.

No union is so intimate, so real, or so perfect, as that of an indwelling life. Think of the life that circulates through a large and fruitful tree. How it penetrates and fills every portion; how inseparably it unites the whole as long as it exists—in wood and leaf, in flower and fruit, everywhere the indwelling life flows and fills. This life is the life of nature, the life of the Spirit of God that dwells in nature. The same life animates our body, the spirit of nature pervading every portion of it with the power of sensibility and action.

Not less intimate, but far more wonderful and real, is the indwelling of the Spirit in the heart of the believer. It is as this indwelling becomes a matter of conscious longing and faith that the soul obeys the command "Then have them make a sanctuary for me, and I will dwell among them" (Exodus 25:8) and experiences the truth of the promise "The place will be consecrated by my glory. . . . Then I will dwell among the Israelites and be their God" (Exodus 29:43, 45).

As the Indwelling One God revealed himself in the Son, whom He sanctified and sent into the world. More than once our Lord insisted, "Don't you believe that I am in the Father, and that the Father is in me? The words I say to you are not just my own. Rather, it is the Father, living in me, who is doing his work" (John 14:10). It is especially as the temple of God that believers are more than once called holy in the New Testament: "We are the temple of the living God" (2 Corinthians 6:16). "Your body is a temple of the Holy Spirit" (1 Corinthians 6:19). "The whole building is joined together and rises to become a holy temple in the Lord" (Ephesians 2:21). It is through the Spirit that the heart is prepared for the indwelling of the Holy Spirit. The measure of His indwelling and His revelation of Christ is the measure of holiness.

We have seen what the various degrees of nearness to God's presence were in Israel. They are still to be found in Christians today. Some Christians dwell in the camp, but know little of drawing close to the Holy One. Outer-court Christians long for pardon and peace. They always come to the altar of atonement, but know little of true nearness or holiness or of their privilege as priests to enter the holy place. There are still others who have learned that this is their calling and long to draw closer, but they rarely understand the boldness they could have to enter into the holiest of all and dwell there. Those to whom this secret of the Lord has been revealed are truly blessed. They know what the rent veil means: access into the immediate presence of the Lord. The veil has been taken away from their hearts and they have found the secret of true holiness.

The God who calls you to holiness is the God of the indwelling life. The tabernacle typifies it, the Son reveals it, the Spirit communicates it, and the eternal glory will fully display it. As a believer, you may experience it. It is your calling to be God's holy temple. Only yield yourself to His indwelling. Do not seek holiness in what you are or *do;* seek it in God alone. Do not even seek it as a gift from

God; seek it in God himself, in His indwelling presence. Worship Him in the beauty of holiness, as He dwells in the high and holy place. And as you worship, listen to His voice: "For this is what the high and lofty One says—he who lives forever, whose name is holy: 'I live in a high and holy place, but also with him who is contrite and lowly in spirit'" (Isaiah 57:15). As the Spirit strengthens us in the inner man so that Christ dwells in our heart by faith, and as the Father comes and together with Him makes His abode in us, it is then that we are holy. In true wholehearted consecration, let us yield ourselves completely to be the habitation of the Holy One, just as were the tabernacle and the temple. A house filled with the glory of God, a heart filled with all the fullness of God, is God's promise; that is our portion. In faith claim and accept and hold fast the blessing: Christ, the Holy One of God, in His Father's name, will enter and take possession of you. Then faith will bring the solution to all our difficulties, the victory over all our failures, and the fulfillment of all our desires. "The place [the heart] will be consecrated by my glory. . . . Then I will dwell among [them]" (Exodus 29:43, 45). The open secret of true holiness, the secret of joy unspeakable, is Christ dwelling in the heart by faith.

We bow our knees to the Father of our Lord Jesus that He would grant unto us, according to the riches of His glory, what He himself has taught us to ask for. We ask that Christ may dwell in our hearts by faith. We long for that most blessed, permanent, conscious indwelling of the Lord Jesus in the heart, which He so distinctly promised as the fruit of the Holy Spirit's coming. Father, we ask for what Christ meant when He spoke of the loving, obedient disciple: "I will come and manifest myself to him. We will come and take up our abode with him." Grant unto us this indwelling of Christ in the heart by faith!

For this, we ask you to strengthen us with might by your Spirit in the inner man. Almighty God, let the spirit of your divine power work mightily within us, renewing our mind, will, and affections, so that the heart is thoroughly prepared and furnished as a temple, as a home for Jesus. Let that blessed Spirit strengthen us to have the faith that receives the blessed Savior and His indwelling presence. We ask it in His name. Amen.

Personal Application

1. God's dwelling in the midst of Israel was the central fact to which all the commands concerning holiness were only preparatory and subordinate. So the work of the Holy Spirit also culminates in the personal indwelling of Christ (John 14:21, 23; Ephesians 3:16–17). Aim at this and expect it.

2. The tabernacle with its three divisions was, as pictured in other spiritual truths, the image of man's threefold nature. Our spirit is the holiest of all, where God is meant to dwell, where the Holy Spirit is given. The life of the soul, with its powers of feeling, knowing, and willing, is the holy place. And the outer life of the body, of conduct and action, is the outer court. Begin by believing that the Spirit dwells in the inmost sanctuary, where His workings are secret and hidden. Honor Him by trusting Him to work, by yielding to Him in silent worship before God. From within He will take possession of our thoughts and will; He will even fill the outer court, the body, with the holiness of God. "The God of peace, sanctify you through and through. May your whole spirit, soul and body be kept blameless. . . . The one who calls you is faithful and he will do it." (1 Thessalonians 5:23–24).

3. God's indwelling was within the veil, in the unseen, the secret place. Faith knew it, and served Him with holy fear. Our faith knows that God the Holy Spirit has His abode in the hidden place of our inner life. Open your inmost being to Him; bow in lowly reverence before the Holy One as you yield yourself to His working. Holiness is the presence of the Indwelling One.

Chapter 9

Holiness and Mediation

Make a plate of pure gold and engrave on it . . . Holy to the Lord. . . . It will be on Aaron's forehead, and he will bear the guilt involved in the sacred gifts the Israelites consecrate, whatever their gifts may be. It will be on Aaron's forehead continually so that they will be acceptable to the Lord.

Exodus 28:36, 38

God's house was to be the dwelling place of His holiness, the place where He was to reveal himself as the Holy One, not to be approached except with fear and reverence; as the One who makes holy, drawing to himself all who would be made partakers of His holiness. The center of the revelation of His holy presence is found in the person of the high priest, in his double capacity of representing God with man and man with God. He is the embodiment of the divine holiness in human form, and of human holiness as a divine gift, as far as the dispensation of symbol and shadow could offer and express it. In him God came near to sanctify and bless the people. In him the people came nearest to God. And yet the very Day of Atonement, in which he might enter into the most holy, was only the proof of how unholy man is and how unfit to abide in God's presence. In himself a proof of Israel's lack of holiness, he still was a type and picture of the coming Savior, our blessed Lord Jesus, and a wonderful exhibition of the way the holiness of God should become the portion of His people.

Among the many points in which the high priest typified Christ as our sanctification, perhaps none is more representative or beautiful than the holy crown he wore on his head. Everything about him was to be holy, even his garments. But in one thing this holiness reached its fullest manifestation. On his forehead he was always to wear a plate of gold engraved with the words *Holy to the Lord*. There everyone read that the whole object of his existence, the one thing for which he lived, was to embody and bear the divine holiness, to be the chosen one through whom God's holiness might flow out in blessing upon the people.

The way in which the blessing of the holy crown was to act was a most remarkable one. In bearing *Holy to the Lord* on his forehead, the priest was "[to] bear the guilt involved in the sacred gifts the Israelites consecrate[d] ... that they [would] be acceptable to the Lord." For every sin some sacrifice or way of atonement had been devised.

But what about the sin that embodied the very sacrifice and religious service itself? "You desire truth in the inner parts" (Psalms 51:6). How painfully the worshiper might be oppressed by the consciousness that his penitence, his faith, his love, his obedience, his very consecration, were all imperfect and defiled! Even for this need God had provided. The holiness of the high priest covered the sin of the worshiper and the unholiness of his holy things. The holy crown was God's pledge that the holiness of the high priest rendered the worshiper acceptable. If he was unholy, there was one who was holy, whose holiness availed for him too. He could look to the high priest not only to effect atonement by his blood sprinkling but also to secure a holiness in his person that made him and his gifts acceptable. Conscious of personal unholiness, the worshiper could rejoice in a mediator, in the holiness of another, the priest whom God had provided.

We have in this picture a most precious lesson, leading us a step further in the way of holiness. God produces holiness through the One whom He has chosen, whose holiness belongs to us as His brethren, the members of His own body. This holiness has such efficacy that the insufficiency of our best intentions is cleansed and we can enter the holy presence with the assurance of being altogether well-pleasing to God.

This is precisely the lesson that many earnest seekers after holiness need. They know all that the Word teaches of the blessed Atonement and the full pardon it has brought. They believe in the Father's wonderful love and what He is ready to do for them. But when they hear of the childlike simplicity and assurance of faith, the loving obedience and blessed surrender with which the Father expects them to come and receive the blessing, their hearts fail for fear—as if the blessing were beyond their reach. It doesn't seem to help when they hear the Holy One is said to come closer when their lack of holiness renders them incapable of claiming or grasping His presence. In God's Son as mediator, holiness is prepared and stored up—enough for *all* who come through Him. As I pray or worship, and realize how much I lack of that humility, fervency, and faith that God has a right to demand, I can look up to the High Priest in His holiness, to the holy crown upon His forehead. The words there help me to believe that the iniquity of my best intentions is borne and taken away. With all my deficiency and unworthiness, I may know most assuredly that my prayer is acceptable, a sweet-smelling savor. I may look up to the Holy One to see Him smiling on me for the sake of His anointed one. The holy crown shall always be on His forehead, that they may be accepted before the Lord. It is the blessed truth of substitution—One for all—and of mediatorship, God's way of making us holy. The sacrifice of the worshiping Israelite is holy and acceptable in virtue of the holiness of Another.

The Old Testament shadow can never adequately set forth the New Testament reality with its fullness of grace and truth. As we proceed in our study, we will find that the holiness of Jesus our sanctification is not only imputed but also imparted because we are in Him; the new man we have put on is created in true holiness. We are not only counted holy but we are holy. We have received a new holy nature in Christ Jesus. "Both the one who makes men holy and those who are made holy are of the same family. So Jesus is not ashamed to call them brothers" (Hebrews 2:11). Our living union with Jesus, God's holy one, has given us the new and holy nature, and with that a claim and a share in all the holiness there is in Jesus. So as often as we are conscious of how unholy we are we have only to come under the covering of the holiness of Jesus to enjoy the full assurance that we, and our gifts, are acceptable. No matter how great the weakness of our faith, the shortcoming in our desire for God's glory, or the lack in our love or zeal, when we see Jesus—with "Holy to the Lord" on His forehead—we lift up our faces to receive the divine smile of full approval and perfect acceptance.

This is God's way of making holy. He begins with the center, Christ, and from Him in an ever-widening circle makes those holy who come to Him. We can be sure that this divine method is crowned with success. In the Word we find a most remarkable illustration of the extent to which it will be realized. We find the words on the holy crown once again in the Old Testament at its close. In the day of the Lord, "*Holy to the Lord* will be inscribed on the bells of the horses" (Zechariah 14:20). The high priest's motto shall then have become the watchword of daily life—every article of beauty or of service shall be holy too, from the head it shall have extended to the skirts of the garments.

Let us begin with realizing the holiness of Jesus in its power to cover the shortcomings of our walk. Let us put it to the test and no longer allow our unworthiness to hold us back or cause us to doubt. Believe that our being and our sanctified choices are acceptable because in Christ they are holy to the Lord. Let us live in this consciousness of acceptance and enter into fellowship with the Holy One. As we enter in and abide in the holiness of Jesus, His holiness will enter and abide in us. It will take possession of us and spread its consuming power through our whole life, until upon everything that belongs to us the words shall be emblazoned: *Holy to the Lord.* Again we shall find how God's way of holiness always starts from a center—here the center of our renewed nature—and then spreads throughout the whole circumference of our being to make His holiness prove its power. Let us but dwell under the covering of the holiness of Jesus as He fills up the lack in our daily walk, and He will make our life and us holy to the Lord.

My God and Father, my soul blesses you for this wonderful revelation of what your way and your grace are with those whom you have called "holy in Christ." You know, Lord, how we have limited the effects of your free acceptance of us by our own attainments and the conscious shortcoming this has wrought. We did not know that in the holiness of Him who makes us holy, there is a divinely infinite efficacy to cover our iniquities and give us the assurance of perfect acceptance. Blessed Father, open our eyes to see and our hearts to understand this holy crown of our blessed Jesus, with its wonderful label, "Holy to the Lord."

When our hearts condemn us because we do not consciously pray according to the will or for the glory of God, or truly in the name of Jesus, then, most Holy Father, be pleased by your Spirit to show us how bright the smile and how hearty the welcome we still have with you. Teach us to come in the holiness of our High Priest and enter into your holiness until it takes possession of us and permeates our whole being, and all that is in us becomes holy to the Lord. Amen.

Personal Application

1. Holiness is not something I can see or admire in myself; rather, it is covering myself and losing myself in the holiness of Jesus. How wonderfully this is typified in Aaron and the holy crown. And the more I see and have apprehended of the holiness of Jesus, the less shall I see or seek holiness in myself.

2. He will make me holy. My temper and disposition will be renewed. My heart and mind cleansed and sanctified. Holiness will be a new nature. All along there will be the consciousness, humbling and yet joyful: It is not I; Christ lives in me.

3. Bow humbly with an open heart before God that the Holy Spirit may reveal to you what it is to be holy in the holiness of Another, in the holiness of Jesus.

4. Do not struggle too much to grasp this with the intellect. Just believe it and look in simplicity and trust to Jesus to make it all right for you.

5. Holy in Christ. In childlike faith I take Christ's holiness afresh as my covering before God. In loving obedience I take it into my will and my life. I trust and I follow Jesus: this is the path to holiness.

6. In our lessons in the Word from the beginning forward, we see that the elements of holiness in us are these, each corresponding to some special aspect of God's holiness: deep restfulness (chap. 3); humble reverence (chap. 4); entire surrender (chap. 5); joyful adoration (chap. 6); simple obedience (chap. 7). These all prepare us for the divine indwelling (chap. 8), and this again we have through abiding in Jesus with the crown of holiness on His head.

— Chapter 10 —

Holiness and Separation

I am the Lord your God, who has set you apart from the nations.
You are to be holy to me because I, the Lord, am holy, and I have
set you apart from the nations to be my own.

Leviticus 20:24, 26

He must be holy until the period of his separation to the Lord is
over. . . . Throughout the period of his separation
he is consecrated to the Lord.

Numbers 6:5, 8

And so Jesus also suffered outside the city gate to make the people
holy through his own blood. Let us, then, go to him outside the
camp, bearing the disgrace he bore.

Hebrews 13:12–13

Separation in itself is not holiness, but it is the way to it. Though there can be no holiness without separation, there can be separation without holiness. It is of deep importance to understand both the difference and the connection that we may be kept from error on the one hand of counting separation alone as holiness, and the error on the other hand of seeking holiness without separation.

The Hebrew word for holiness possibly comes from a root word that means to separate. But where the translation is "separate" or "sever" or "set apart," we have quite different words. The word for holy is used exclusively to express that specific idea. Although the idea of holy always includes that of separation, it is itself something infinitely higher. It is important to understand this well, because being set apart to God, surrender to His claim, and devotion or consecration to His service are often spoken of as if these constituted holiness. We cannot too strongly emphasize that these are only the beginning, the presupposition—holiness itself is infinitely more. It is not what I am or do or give that makes me holy but what God is and gives and does in me. God's taking possession of me makes me holy; it is the presence and the glory of God that makes holy.

A careful study of God's words to Israel will make this clear to us. In Leviticus alone there are three direct references to our holiness and God's holiness. Holiness is the highest attribute of God, expressive not only of His relationship to Israel but also of His very being and nature, His infinite moral perfection. Only by very slow and gradual steps can He teach the carnal, darkened mind of man what this means, yet from the very beginning He tells His people that His purpose is that they should be like Him—holy—because He is holy. To tell me that God separates men for himself to be His—even as He gives himself to be theirs—tells me of a relationship that exists but tells me nothing of the real nature of this holy being or of the essential worth of the holiness He will communicate to me. Separation is only the setting apart and taking possession of the vessel to be cleansed and used; it is the filling of the vessel with the precious contents we entrust to it that gives it its real value. Holiness is the divine filling of that vessel without which the separation leaves us empty. So again, separation is not holiness.

But separation is essential to holiness. "I am the Lord your God, who has set you apart from the nations." Until I have chosen and separated a vessel from those around it, and cleansed it, if need be, I cannot fill or use it. I must have it in my hand with full and exclusive command of it, or I will not pour into it the precious milk or wine. In that way God separated His people unto himself when He brought them up out of Egypt, when He gave them His covenant and His law so that He might work out His purpose of making them holy. This He could not do until He had taken them aside and awakened in them the consciousness that they were His people, wholly and only His, until He had taught them also to separate themselves unto Him.

The institution of the Nazarite will confirm this and will also bring out very clearly what separation means. Israel was meant to be a holy nation. Its holiness was especially typified in its priests. With regard to the individual Israelite, we nowhere read in the books of Moses of his being holy. But there were ordinances through which the Israelite who wanted to prove his desire to be entirely holy could do so. He might separate himself from the ordinary life of the nation around him and live the life of a Nazarite, a separated one. In those days of shadow and type, this separation was accepted as holiness. "Throughout the period of his separation he is consecrated to the Lord."

The separation especially consisted of three things: *temperance*, in abstinence from the fruit of the vine; *humiliation*, in not cutting or shaving his hair ("If a man has long hair, it is a disgrace to him" (1 Corinthians 11:14); *self-sacrifice*, in not defiling himself for even father or mother upon their death. What we must particularly note is that the separation was not from things unlawful but things lawful. There was nothing sinful in itself in Abraham's living in his father's house or in Israel's dwelling in Egypt. The spirit of separation is manifested in giving up not only what can be proved to be sinful but also all that may hinder our surrender into God's hands to make us holy.

Separation is not an arbitrary demand of God but has its ground in the very nature of things. To separate something is to set it free for a special use or purpose that it may fulfill the will of the one who chose it and so realize its destiny. It is the principle that lies at the root of all division of labor; complete separation to one branch of study or work is the path to success and perfection. By illustration, imagine an oak forest with its trees shooting straight upward and close together. On the outskirts of the forest, one tree is separated from the others and its heavy trunk and wide-spreading branches prove that being separated and having a large piece of ground to itself, where roots and branches can spread, is the secret of growth and greatness. Our human powers are limited; if God is to take full possession of them and if we are to enjoy Him fully, separation to Him is nothing but the simple, natural, indispensable requisite. God wants us for himself that He may give himself completely to us.

The purpose of separation is clear: "You are to be holy to me because I, the Lord, am holy, and I have set you apart from the nations to be my own." In the deepest sense of the word, God has separated us for himself that He might enter into our innermost being and reveal himself to us. His holiness is the sum and the center of His perfection. Separation never has value in itself; in fact, it may become wrong or hurtful—everything depends upon the purpose in mind. It is as God takes full possession of us, as the eternal life in Christ has mastery of our whole being, and the Holy Spirit flows fully and freely through us so that we dwell in God and God in us, that separation will be a spiritual reality. As we see, accept, and follow after this purpose of God, difficult questions as to what we must be separated from and how much sacrifice separation demands will be easier to answer. God separates us from all that does not lead us into His holiness and fellowship.

Beyond the purpose of separation, we must recognize the power of separation. One of the first words a child learns is the word *mine*. For the child it may refer to his toys; to the honest laborer it speaks of gains and rewards; to the patriot who would die for his country it means ownership of homeland and freedom. "Mine" sets something apart from everything else. It is a word that love speaks, whether by a child to his mother or a mother to her child. It is the word of the bridegroom to his bride and the bride to her bridegroom. And most important, it is the word God uses when He speaks of His dear children: "Fear not, for I have redeemed you; I have summoned you by name; you are mine" (Isaiah 43:1). It is always with the word *mine* that love exerts its magnetic power to draw the object of its affection to itself. God himself knows no better argument or more powerful attraction than this: to call His children His own. The power of separation will come to us and work in us just as fully as we yield ourselves to study and realize its holy purpose, to listen for and appropriate the wonderful gift of belonging.

Divine love does its separating work step by step along a glorious path. In redemption it prepares the way. Israel was separated from Egypt by the blood of the Lamb and by the guiding pillars of fire and cloud. In the command "Come out from them and be separate" (2 Corinthians 6:17), man is awakened to action. In the promise "I will be your God" (Exodus 6:7), desire is stirred and faith strengthened. In all the holy saints and servants of God—and at last in Him who was holy, harmless, undefiled, and separate from sinners—love points the way. In the power of the Holy Spirit, the Spirit of holiness, it seals the separation by the presence of the indwelling God.

"How will anyone know that you are pleased with me and with your people unless you go with us?" said Moses. "What else will distinguish me and your people from all the other people on the face of the earth?" (Exodus 33:16). The consciousness of God's indwelling presence, making and keeping us His very own, works true separation from the world and its spirit, from ourselves and our own will. As we accept this separation, the holiness of God will enter and take possession. Then we will realize that to be the Lord's property signifies infinitely more than to be acknowledged as His—it means that God by the power and indwelling of the Holy Spirit, fills our being, our affections, and our will, with His own life and holiness. He separates us for himself and sanctifies us to be His dwelling place.

O my God, who has separated me for yourself, I ask you by your mighty power to make this divine separation real to me. Within the depths of my own spirit, and without, in all my relationships, may the crown of separation of my God be upon me.

I pray especially that you would perfect in me a true separation from self! Let your presence by the indwelling of my Lord Jesus be the power that banishes self from the throne. I have turned from it with abhorrence. Father, reveal your Son fully in me! It is His enthronement in my heart that can keep me as your own.

In my outward life, Lord, give me grace to wait for divine wisdom, to know how to witness for your glory and to meet the needs of your people. Give me grace for the blessedness of a complete surrender of everything to God, a separation that holds back nothing, to be His and His alone.

Holy Lord God, visit your people. Withdraw them from the world and from conformity to it. Separate, Lord, your own for yourself. Separate the wheat from the chaff; separate as by fire the gold from the dross so that it may be seen who are the Lord's, His holy ones. Amen.

Personal Application

1. Love separates effectually. With what jealousy a husband claims his wife, a mother her children, a miser his possessions! Pray that

the Holy Spirit may show how God brought you to himself that you should be His. He is a holy God; He is a jealous God. God's love shed abroad in the heart makes separation easy.

2. Death separates effectually. If I reckon myself to be dead in Christ, I am separated from self by the power of Christ's death. Life separates still more mightily. As I say, "I no longer live, but Christ lives in me" (Galatians 2:20), I am lifted up out of the life of self.

3. Separation must be visible. It is meant as a witness to others and ourselves. It must find expression in the external if internally it is to be real and strong. It is the characteristic of a symbolic act that it not merely expresses a feeling but nourishes and strengthens the feeling to which it corresponds. When the soul enters the fellowship of God, it feels the need of external separation, sometimes even from what appears to others to be harmless. If motivated by the spirit of consecration to God, external separation can only be strengthening to the soul.

4. Separation unto God and appropriation by Him go together. This has been the blessing that has come to martyrs, confessors, missionaries—all who have forsaken all.

5. Separation begins in love and ends in love. The spirit of separation is the spirit of self-sacrifice, of surrender to the love of God. The truly separate one will be the most loving and the most gracious, yielded to serve God and man. That which separated and distinguished Jesus from all others was His self-sacrificing love. It is through this kind of self-sacrifice that we are to be made like Him.

6. One aspect of God's holiness is His separateness. Let us enter into His separateness from the world; it will enhance our holiness. Unite yourself with God. God separates us not by an act from without, but as His will and presence take possession of us.

The Holy One of Israel

I am the Lord who brought you up out of Egypt to be your God;
therefore be holy, because I am holy. . . . Consider
them holy, because I the Lord am holy.

Leviticus 11:45; 21:8

I am the Lord, your God, the Holy One of Israel, your Savior. . . .
I am the Lord, your Holy One, Israel's Creator, your King.

Isaiah 43:3, 15

Exodus shows God making provision for the holiness of His people. In the holy times and holy places, He taught His people that everything around Him must be holy. He would dwell only in the midst of holiness. His people must be a holy people. But there is no direct mention of God himself as holy. In the book of Leviticus we are led a step further. Here for the first time God speaks of His own holiness and makes it the plea for the holiness of His people as well as its pledge and power. Without this the revelation of holiness would be incomplete and the call to holiness powerless. True holiness will come to us as we learn that God alone is holy. He alone makes us holy. Only as we come to Him and in obedience and love are linked to Him can His holiness rest on us.

From the books of Moses onward we find that the name of God as holy is seldom found in the inspired writings until we come to Isaiah, the evangelist prophet. There it occurs twenty-six times, its true meaning revealed by how it is linked with the names of Savior and Redeemer. The sentiments of joy and trust and praise with which a redeemed people would look upon their Deliverer are all mentioned in connection with the name of the Holy One.

"Shout aloud and sing for joy, people of Zion, for great is the Holy One of Israel among you" (Isaiah 12:6). "The needy will rejoice in the Holy One of Israel" (Isaiah 29:19). "You will rejoice in the Lord and glory in the Holy One of Israel" (Isaiah 41:16).

In the beginning we saw that God the Creator was God the Sanctifier, perfecting the work of His hands. In Israel we saw that God the Redeemer was God the Sanctifier, making holy the people He had chosen for himself. Here in Isaiah we see how God the Sanctifier is to bring about the great redemption of the New Testament: the Holy One is the Redeemer. God redeems because He is holy and loves to make holy: holiness will be redemption perfected. Redemption and holiness together are to be found in the personal relationship to God. The key to the secret of holiness is offered to each believer in the word "This is what the Lord says—your Redeemer, the Holy One of Israel: 'I am the Lord your God' " (Isaiah 48:17). To come near, to know, to possess the Holy One and be possessed of Him is true holiness.

If God's holiness is the only hope for ours, it is reasonable that we seek to know what that holiness is. Although we may find it to be something that is beyond our understanding, it will be helpful to see what has been revealed in the Word concerning it. Let us do so in the spirit of holy fear and worship, trusting the Holy Spirit to be our teacher.

First, notice how this holiness of God—though often mentioned as one of the divine attributes—can hardly be considered on the same level with the others. The other attributes all refer to some special aspect or characteristic of the divine nature; holiness appears to express the very essence or perfection of His being. None of the attributes can describe all that belongs to God; but Scripture uses the word *holy* to describe His name, His day, His habitation, His Word. In the word *holy* we have the nearest possible summary of all the divine perfections, the description of what Divinity is. For this reason theologians have found difficulty in framing a definition that can express all that the word implies.

The original Hebrew word (whether derived from a root signifying to separate or another with the idea of shining) expressed the idea of something distinguished from others, separate from them by superior excellence. God is separate and different from all that is created. He keeps himself separate from all that is not of God. As the Holy One, He maintains His divine glory and perfection against whatever might interfere with it. "There is no one holy like the Lord" (1 Samuel 2:2); " 'To whom will you compare me? Or who is my equal?' says the Holy One" (Isaiah 40:25). In referring to His holiness, God is indeed the Incomparable One; holiness is His alone; there is nothing like it in heaven or earth, except when He gives it. So our holiness will consist not in a human separation in which we attempt to imitate God's holiness, but rather in entering into His separateness, belonging entirely to Him, set apart by Him for himself.

Closely connected with this is the idea of exaltation: "This is what the high and lofty One says ... whose name is holy" (Isaiah 57:15). It was the Holy One who was seen sitting upon a throne high and lifted up, the object of the worship of the seraphim. In Psalm 99 God's holiness is especially connected with His exaltation. For this reason, too, His holiness is often linked with His glory and majesty. Here our holiness will be revealed as the poverty and humility that comes when "the arrogance of man [is] brought low and the pride of men humbled; the Lord alone will be exalted in that day" (Isaiah 2:17).

If we ask what comprises the infinite excellence of this separation and exaltation, we think of divine purity, not only in its negative aspect as hatred of sin but also with the more positive element of perfect beauty. Because we are sinners and the revelation of God's holiness is in a world of sin, it is natural and right that the first and abiding impression of God's holiness should be that of an infinite purity that cannot look upon sin, in whose presence the sinner can only hide his face and tremble. The righteousness of God, forbidding and condemning and punishing sin, has its root in His holiness and is one of its two elements—the devouring and destroying power of the consuming fire. "The holy God will show himself holy by his righteousness" (Isaiah 5:16); in righteousness the holiness of the Holy One is maintained and revealed.

Light not only discovers what is impure that it may be purified but is in itself a thing of infinite beauty. Some of the holiest men have not hesitated to speak of God's holiness as the infinite beauty of the Divine Being, the perfect purity and essence of that light in which God dwells. If the holiness of God is to become ours, to rest upon and enter into us, there must be a holy fear of sin, an aversion to all that would grieve our holy God. Side by side and in perfect harmony with that fear will be the deep longing to behold the beauty of the Lord, an admiration of His divine glory and a joyful surrender to be His alone.

We must go one step further. When God says, "I am holy: I make holy," we see that one of the chief elements of His holiness is to communicate itself, to allow others to partake of its perfection and blessedness. This is love. In the wonderful revelation in Isaiah of what the Holy One is to His people, we must beware of misreading God's precious Word. It does not say that although God is the Holy One and hates sin and ought to punish and destroy all who sin, He nonetheless saves. Rather, we are taught that because He is the Holy One, who delights to make holy, He will be the deliverer of His people (see Hosea 11:9). It is holiness above all else that we are invited to look to, to trust in, and to rejoice in. The Holy One is the One who makes holy. He redeems and saves so that He may win our confidence, that He may draw us to himself, so that in our personal relationship to Him we will learn to obey and become of one mind with Him, holy as He is holy.

Divine holiness is that infinite perfection of Divinity in which righteousness and love are in perfect harmony. It is that energy of the divine life by which God not only keeps himself free from all creature weakness or sin but also unceasingly seeks to lift the creature into union with himself and into full participation of His own purity and perfection. The glory of God as God, as the God of creation and redemption, is His holiness. It is in this that the separateness and exaltation of God, even above man's comprehension, truly consists. God is light (John 1:5); in His infinite purity He reveals all darkness and yet has no fellowship with it. He judges and condemns it; He saves out of it and lifts up into the fellowship of His own purity and blessedness. This is the Holy One of Israel.

It is this God who speaks to us, "I am the Lord your God; I am holy; I make holy." It is in the adoring contemplation of His holiness, in the trustful surrender to it, in the loving fellowship with himself, the Holy One, that we can be made holy.

Do you want to be holy? Come and claim Him as your God, as the One who can make you holy. Only remember that holiness is himself. Come to Him; worship Him; give Him glory. Let self be abased and be content that holiness belongs to Him; He alone can give it. As His presence fills your heart, as His holiness and glory are your delight—as the Holy One becomes all in all to you—you will be holy with the holiness He loves to impart. And as you see nothing to admire in yourself but only beauty in Him, you will know that

He has laid His glory on you; your holiness is found in the song "There is no one holy like the Lord" (1 Samuel 2:2).

O God, we have again heard the wonderful revelation of yourself, "I am holy." As we saw how infinitely exalted your holiness is above our concept of it, we heard your call—almost more wonderful—"Be holy, as I am holy." But as every thought of how we were to be holy as you are holy dismayed us, we heard your voice once again, in this most wonderful word of all: "I make you holy."

Help us to realize how unholy we are so that we may take the place that is fitting in your presence. Reveal the sinfulness of our nature and all that is of self so that it may no longer be possible to live in it! May the light that reveals this also reveal how your holiness is our only hope, our sure refuge, and our complete deliverance. O Lord, speak by your Spirit to our innermost being the realization that you alone, our Redeemer, are holy. And may our faith grow into the assured confidence that we can be holy too.

Lord God, we wait for you; reveal yourself in power within us and fit us to be messengers of your holiness, to tell your people how holy you are, how holy we must be, and how holy you will make us. Amen.

Personal Application

1. This Holy One is God Almighty. Before He revealed himself to Israel as the Holy One, He made himself known to Abraham as the Almighty "who gives life to the dead" (Romans 4:17). In all your dealings with God for holiness, remember He is the Almighty One who can do wonders in you. Say often, "To him who is able to do immeasurably more than all we ask or imagine . . . to him be glory" (Ephesians 3:20–21).

2. This Holy One, the righteous God, is a consuming fire. Cast yourself into Him, so that all that is sinful may be consumed. As you lay yourself upon the altar, expect the fire. "Offer the parts

of your body to him as instruments of righteousness" (Romans 6:13).

3. This Holy One is the God of love. He is your Father; yield yourself to Him; let the Holy Spirit cry in you, "Abba, Father!" That is, let Him fill your heart with God's father-love. God's holiness is His fatherliness; our holiness is childlikeness. Be simple, loving, trustful.

4. This Holy One is God. Let Him be God to you: ruling all, filling all, working all. Worship Him, come near to Him, live with and in and for Him: He will be your holiness.

Chapter 12

The Thrice-Holy One

*I saw the Lord seated on a throne, high and exalted. . . . Above
him were seraphs . . . and they were calling to one another:
"Holy, holy, holy is the Lord Almighty; the whole earth
is full of his glory."*

Isaiah 6:1–3

*The four living creatures. . . . Day and night they never stop saying:
"Holy, holy, holy is the Lord God Almighty, who was,
and is, and is to come."*

Revelation 4:8

Not only on earth but also in heaven is the holiness of God His chief
and most glorious attribute. And not only on earth but also in
heaven the highest inspiration of adoration and praise mentions His
holiness. The brightest of living beings, they who are ever before and
around and above the throne, find their glory in adoring and pro-
claiming the holiness of God. Surely for us too there can be no
higher honor than to study and know, to worship and adore, to
proclaim and show forth the glory of the Thrice-Holy One.

After Moses, Isaiah was the chief messenger of the holiness of
God. Each of them had a special preparation for his commission to

make known the Holy One. Moses saw the Holy One in the fire, and hid his face and feared to look upon God, and so was prepared to be His messenger and to praise Him as "glorious in holiness" (Exodus 3). Isaiah heard the song of the seraphim, saw the fire on the altar and the house filled with the smoke, and he cried out, "Woe is me!" In the deep sense of the need of cleansing, he received the touch of the fire and the purging of his sin (Isaiah 6). Only then might he bear to Israel the gospel of the Holy One as its redeemer. May it be in the spirit of fear and lowly worship that we listen to the song of the seraphim and seek to know and worship the Thrice-Holy One. May we too be cleansed with fire that we may be found fit to tell God's people that He is the Holy One of Israel, their redeemer.

The threefold repetition of *holy* by the church of Christ has at all times been connected with the Holy Trinity. The song of the living creatures around the throne (Revelation 4) is evidence of this. There we find it followed by the adoration of Him who was and is and is to come, the Almighty: the Eternal Source, the present manifestation in the Son, the future perfecting of the revelation of God in the Spirit's work in His church. The truth of the Holy Trinity is often regarded as an abstract doctrine with little direct bearing on practical life. So far is this from being the case that a living faith must be rooted in it. Some spiritual insight into the relationship and the operation of each of the Three and the reality of their living oneness is an essential element of true growth in knowledge and spiritual understanding. Let us here regard the Trinity especially in its relation to God's holiness and as the source of ours. What does it mean that we adore the Thrice-Holy One? God is not only holy but also makes His people holy: in the revelation of the three persons we have the revelation of the way in which God makes us holy.

The Trinity teaches us that God has revealed himself in two ways. The Son is the form of God, His manifestation as He shows himself to man, the image in which His unseen glory is embodied and to which man is to be conformed. The Spirit is the power of God working in man and leading him into that image. In Jesus, He who had been in the form of God took the form of man, and the Divine Holiness was literally manifested in the form of a human life and the members of a human body. A new holy human nature was formed in Christ to be communicated to us. In His death, His own personal holiness was perfected as human obedience, and so the power of sin was conquered and broken. Therefore, in the Resurrection, through the Spirit of holiness, He was declared to be the Son of God with power to impart His life to us. There the Spirit of holiness was set free from the veil of the flesh, the restraints that hindered it, and obtained power to enter and dwell in man. The Holy Spirit was poured out as the fruit of the Resurrection and the Ascension. Now the Spirit is the power of God in us, working upward toward Christ to reproduce His life and holiness in us, to fit us for fully receiving Him and showing Him forth in our lives. Christ from above comes to us as the embodiment of the unseen holiness of God: the Spirit from within lifts us up to meet Him and fits us to receive and make our own all that is in Him.

The Triune God whom we adore is the Thrice-Holy One. The mystery of the Trinity is the mystery of holiness. The glory and the power of the Trinity are the glory and power of God, who makes us holy. There is God dwelling in light inaccessible, a consuming fire of holy love, destroying all that resists, glorifying into its own purity all that yields. There is the Son, casting himself into that consuming fire—whether in its eternal blessedness in heaven or its angry wrath on earth—a willing sacrifice to be its food and its satisfaction as well as the revelation of its power to destroy and to save. And there is the Spirit of holiness, the flames of that mighty fire spreading on every side, convicting and judging as the Spirit of burning, and then transforming into its own brightness and holiness all that it can reach. All the relationships of the three persons to each other and to us have their root and their meaning in the revelation of God as the Holy One. As we know and partake of Him we shall know and partake of holiness.

How shall we know Him? Let us learn to know the holiness of God as the seraphs do: in the worship of the Thrice-Holy One. With veiled faces let us join in the ceaseless song of adoration: "Holy, holy, holy, is the Lord of hosts." Each time we meditate on the Word, each prayer we make to the Holy God, each act of faith in Christ, the Holy One, each exercise of waiting dependence upon the Holy Spirit, let it all be in the spirit of worship.

Let us learn to know the holiness of God as Isaiah did. He was to be the chosen messenger to reveal and interpret to the people the name, the Holy One of Israel. His preparation was the vision that made him cry out, "Woe to me! . . . My eyes have seen the King, the Lord Almighty" (Isaiah 6:5). Let us bow in silence before the Holy One. Let us feel the cleansing fire from the altar, the touch of the live coals of His holiness, which not only consumes but purges lips and hearts to say, "Here am I, send me" (Isaiah 6:8).

Let us worship, whether like the adoring seraphim or the trembling prophet, until we know that our service is accepted, to tell forth the praise of the Thrice-Holy One.

If we are indeed to be the messengers of the Holy One, let us seek to enter fully into what "thrice-holy" means. *Holy, the Father:* God above us, high and lifted up, whom no man has seen or can see, whose holiness none dare approach, but who himself draws near in His holiness to make holy. *Holy, the Son:* God with us, revealing divine holiness in human life, maintaining it amid the suffering of death for us, and preparing a holy life and nature for His people. *Holy, the Spirit:* God in us, the power of holiness within us, reaching out to and embracing Christ, and transforming our inner life into the union and communion with Him in whom we are holy.

This is perfect holiness—the divine Thrice-Holy: holiness hidden and unapproachable, holiness manifested in human nature, holiness communicated and made our own.

The mystery of the Holy Trinity is the mystery of the Christian life, the mystery of holiness. The three are one, and we need to enter ever more deeply into the truth that none of the three ever works separately or independently of the others. The Son reveals the Father and the Father reveals the Son. The Father gives not himself but the Spirit: the Spirit speaks not of himself but cries, "Abba, Father!" The Son is our sanctification, our life, our all: the fullness is in Him. And yet we must always bow our knees to the Father for Him to reveal Christ in us, for Him to establish us in Christ. The Father does not do this without the Spirit; we have to ask to be strengthened mightily by the Spirit that Christ may dwell in us. Christ gives the Spirit to them that believe and love and obey; the Spirit again gives Christ, formed within and dwelling in the heart. So in each act of worship, each step of growth, each blessed experience of grace, all three persons are actively engaged. The one is ever three; the three are ever one.

To apply this in the life of holiness, faith in the Holy Trinity must be a living practical reality:

In every prayer to the Father to sanctify you, take up your position in Christ, and do it in the power of the Spirit within you.

In every exercise of faith in Christ as your sanctification, let your posture be that of prayer to the Father and trust in Him as He delights to honor the Son; and of quiet expectancy of the Spirit's working, through whom the Father glorifies the Son.

In every surrender of the soul to the sanctification of the Spirit, to His leading as the Spirit of holiness, look to the Father, who grants His mighty working and who sanctifies through faith in the Son. Expect the Spirit's power to manifest itself in showing the will of God and Jesus as your sanctification.

If for a time this appears to contradict the simplicity of childlike faith and prayer, be assured that as God has thus revealed himself, He will also teach you to worship and believe. Then the praise "holy, holy, holy" will become the undertone of all our worship and all our life.

Children of God, called to be holy as He is holy, let us bow down and worship in His holy presence! Come with veiled faces. Turn away from gazing at that which is beyond your comprehension and let the soul be gathered into that inner stillness in which the worship of the heavenly sanctuary alone can be heard. Come, and cover your feet. Withdraw from the busyness of work—be it secular or spiritual—and learn to worship. Come and fall down in self-abasement to let the glory of the Holy One shine upon you. And as you hear and join in singing the song "Holy, holy, holy," you will discover that in such knowledge and worship of the Thrice-Holy One is the power that makes you holy.

Holy, holy, holy, the Lord God Almighty! which was and is and is to come! I worship you as the Triune God. With face veiled and feet covered, I would bow in deep humility and silence, till your mercy lifts me as on eagles' wings to behold your glory.

Most merciful God, who has called me to be holy as you are holy, reveal to me your holiness! As it shines upon me and strikes death to the flesh, may even the most involuntary taint of sin and its slightest manifestation become unbearable. As it shines and revives the hope of being partaker of your holiness, may the confidence grow strong that you are making me holy and will make me a messenger of your holiness.

Thrice-holy God, I worship you as my God. Holy is the Father, holy and making holy, sending His Son into the world that we might behold the very glory of God in a human face, even the face of Jesus Christ.

May even now the worship of heaven that rests neither day nor

*night be the worship my soul renders to you without ceasing. May its
song be, from the depths of my heart, the keynote of my life. Amen.*

Personal Application

1. Thought always needs to distinguish and separate: in life alone
   there is perfect unity. The more we know the living God, the
   more we will realize how truly the Three are One. In each act of
   one person the other two are present. There is not a prayer that
   rises but the presence of the Holy Three is needed: through
   Christ, in the Spirit, we speak to the Father.

2. To apprehend this in faith is to have the secret of holiness. The
   Holy Father above us, ever giving and working; the Holy Son of
   God, the living gift, who has possession of us, in whom we are;
   the Holy Spirit, God within us, through whom the Father works
   and the Son is revealed: this is the God who says, "I am holy, and
   I make holy." In the perfect unity of the work of the three, holiness is found.

3. No wonder the love of the Father and the grace of the Son do
   not accomplish more, when the fellowship of the Holy Spirit is
   little understood, sought after, or accepted. The Holy Spirit is the
   fruit and crown of the divine revelation, through whom the Son
   and the Father come to us. If you would know God, if you would
   be holy, you must be taught and led of the Spirit of God.

4. Whenever you worship the Thrice-Holy One, listen until the
   voice is heard: "Whom shall I send, and who will go for us?" Let
   your answer rise, "Here am I, send me," and offer yourself to be
   a messenger of the holiness of God to those around you.

5. When in meditation and worship you have tried to take in and
   express what God's Word has taught you, confess that you know
   nothing and wait on God to reveal himself.

Chapter 13

Holiness and Humility

For this is what the high and lofty One says—he who lives forever, whose name is holy: "I live in a high and holy place, but also with him who is contrite and lowly in spirit, to revive the spirit of the lowly and to revive the heart of the contrite."

Isaiah 57:15

The revelation we have in Isaiah of God, the Holy One, as the Redeemer and the Savior of His people is very wonderful. In the midst of the people whom He created and formed for himself He dwells as the Holy One, showing forth His power and His glory and filling them with joy and gladness. All these promises, however, refer to the people as a whole. Our text today reveals a new and especially beautiful feature of divine holiness in its relationship to the individual. The high and lofty One, whose name is Holy and whose only fit dwelling place is eternity, looks to the one who is of a humble and contrite heart; with that one will He dwell. God's holiness is His condescending love. It is a consuming fire against all who exalt themselves before Him, but to the spirit of the humble it is like the shining of the sun, heart-reviving and life-giving.

The deep significance of this promise comes out clearly when we connect it with the other promises of New Testament times. The great feature of the new covenant, in its superiority to the old, is that whereas in the law and its institution all was external, in the new the kingdom of God would be within. God's laws are given and written on the heart, a new spirit is put within us, God's own Spirit is given to dwell within our spirit, and so the heart and the inner life are fitted to be the temple and home of God. These constitute the peculiar privileges of the ministration of the Spirit. Our text is perhaps the only one in the Old Testament in which this indwelling of the Holy One—not only among the people but also in the heart of the individual believer—is clearly brought out. In this the two aspects of divine holiness would reach their full manifestation: "I dwell in the high and holy place, and with him also that is of a contrite and humble spirit." In His heaven above, the high and lofty place, and in our heart, contrite and humble, God makes His home. God's holiness is His glory that separates Him by an infinite distance, not only from sin but also from the creature, lifting Him high above it. God's holiness is His love, drawing Him down to the sinner so that He may lift him into His fellowship and likeness and make him holy, as He is holy. The Holy One seeks the humble; the humble find the Holy One. Such are the two lessons we must learn.

The Holy One seeks the humble. Nothing has such an attraction for God and such affinity with holiness as a contrite and humble spirit. The reason is evident. There is no law in the natural or the spiritual world simpler than that two bodies cannot occupy the same space at the same time. In man, self has possession and self-will the mastery—there is no room for God. Only to the extent that the new occupant can empty the space of what it was once filled with can it truly take possession. It is impossible for God to dwell or rule when self is on the throne. Sin and self-love have a blinding influence, and often the believer is not truly conscious of the extent to which self-will reigns. Until it is revealed by God's Spirit, there can be no true contrition or humility. But when the soul sees how self has kept God out, it is broken down with shame and longs to break utterly away from self that God may have His place. This brokenness, and continued breaking down, is expressed by the word *contrition*. When the soul sees how guilty it has been of honoring self and keeping the Holy One from the place to which He alone has a right, it casts itself down in self-abasement and desires to be nothing, giving God the place and the praise that is due His name.

Such humiliation is painful. Its reality consists in the fact that the soul can see nothing in itself in which to trust or hope. And least of all can it imagine that it could be a fit vessel for the divine blessing. But this is the message the Word of the Lord brings to our faith. It tells us that the Holy One, who dwells in the high and lofty place, is seeking and preparing for himself a dwelling here on earth. It tells us something the truly contrite and humble soul could never imagine and hardly believe, that it is with such people, and only such, that God will dwell. These are they in whom God can be glorified, in whom there is room for Him to take the place of self. The Holy One seeks the humble. Just when we see that there is nothing in us to admire or rest in, God sees in us everything to admire and to rest in because there is room for himself. The lowly one is the home of the Holy One.

The humble find the Holy One. Just when the consciousness of sin and weakness and the discovery of how much self there is makes you fear that you can never be holy, the Holy One gives you himself. Not as you look at yourself to know whether you are contrite and humble, but when you are no longer looking at self because you have given up all hope of seeing anything in you but sin, and you look up to the Holy One, you will see how His promise is your only hope. It is by faith that the Holy One is revealed to the contrite soul. Faith is always the opposite of what we see and feel; it looks to God alone. Faith allows the contrite to believe—even in his deepest consciousness of unholiness and fear that he never can be holy—that

God, the Holy One who makes holy, is near to him as his Redeemer and Savior. The contrite is content to be humble, in the consciousness of unworthiness and emptiness, and still rejoices in the assurance that God himself takes possession and revives the heart. Happy the soul who is willing to learn the lesson early that we will always have the simultaneous experience of weakness and power, of emptiness and filling, of deep humiliation as well as the most wonderful indwelling of the Holy One.

This is indeed the deep mystery of the divine life. To human reason it is a paradox. When Paul said of himself, "dying, and yet we live on . . . sorrowful, yet always rejoicing . . . having nothing, and yet possessing everything" (2 Corinthians 6:9–10), he was only giving expression to the law of the kingdom: *as self is displaced and man becomes nothing, God will become all.* Side by side with the deepest sense of nothingness and weakness, a sense of infinite riches and joy unspeakable can fill the heart. However deep and blessed the experience of the indwelling of the Holy Spirit, it is never an indwelling in the old self but a divine presence that humbles self and makes a place for God alone to be exalted. The power of Christ's death and the fellowship of His cross work side by side with the power and the joy of His resurrection. "He who humbles himself will be exalted" (Luke 14:11); in the blessed life of faith, humiliation and exaltation are simultaneous, each dependent on the other.

The humble find the Holy One, and when they have found Him, the possession only humbles them more. It isn't that there is no danger or temptation of the flesh to exalt itself, but knowing the danger, the humble soul seeks for grace to cling more firmly to God alone. Never imagine for a moment that you ever attain a state in which self or the flesh is absolutely dead. Rather, by faith you enter into and abide in a fellowship with Jesus in which self and flesh are crucified. Abiding in Him, you are free from their power—but only as you believe and dwell in Jesus. Therefore, the more abundant

God's grace becomes and the more blessed the indwelling of the Holy Spirit, the more humble we must remain. The more we acknowledge our helplessness without Him, the bolder we will be to claim the victory.

Those of you who profess to be nothing and who trust in grace alone, listen to this glorious message: The One whose name is Holy and who lives in a holy place seeks to dwell in us here on earth. Will you not give Him this joy? Will you not fall down in the dust that He may find in you the humble heart He loves to indwell? Will you believe Him for this? He delights to make His dwelling place in you. "Blessed are the poor in spirit, for theirs is the kingdom" (Matthew 5:3); with them the King dwells. This is the path to holiness: be humble, and the holy nearness and presence of God in you will be your holiness. As you hear the command "Be holy, as I am holy," by faith claim the promise and answer, "I will be holy, O Most Holy God, if you, the Holy One, will dwell with me."

O Lord, you are the high and lofty One, whose name is Holy. And still you say, "I live in a high and holy place, but also with him who is contrite and lowly in spirit." Yes, Lord, when the soul takes the lowest place, and when it feels it is nothing, you love to come and comfort and to dwell with that soul and revive it.

O God! My emptiness humbles me. My many transgressions humble me. My innate sinfulness humbles me. But what humbles me most of all is your infinite condescension and the ineffable indwelling you so graciously offer. Christ bearing our sin, your holy love bearing with our humanity and consenting to dwell in us—this love that passes knowledge is humbling beyond words.

Holy Lord God! Humble me in your presence. Long ago you met your servants and showed yourself to them until they fell upon their faces. My God, you know I have nothing I can bring to you but myself. In my blessed Savior, who humbled himself and became a servant even unto the death of the cross, I hide myself. In Him, in His Spirit and likeness, I would live before you. Work in me, by your Holy Spirit, and as I am crucified to self, let your holy indwelling revive and quicken me. Amen.

Personal Application

1. Lowliness and holiness. Hold fast the intimate connection. Lowliness is taking the place that becomes me; holiness is giving God the place that becomes Him. If I am nothing before Him, and God is all to me, I am in the certain path of holiness. Lowliness becomes holiness when it gives all the glory to God.

2. "Blessed are the poor in spirit, for theirs is the kingdom of heaven." These first words of the Master when He opened His lips to proclaim the kingdom are often the last in the hearts of His disciples. "The kingdom is in the Holy Spirit"; to the poor in spirit, those who know they have nothing that is truly spiritual, the Holy Spirit comes. The poor in spirit are the kingdom of the saints: in them the Holy Spirit reveals the King.

3. Many strive to be humble before God, but with men they maintain their rights and nourish self. Remember that the great school of humility before God is to accept the humbling of man. Christ sanctified himself by accepting the humiliation and injustice that evil men laid upon Him.

4. Humility never sees its own beauty because it refuses to look to itself; it only wonders at the condescension of the Holy God and rejoices in the humility of Jesus.

5. The link between holiness and humbleness is indwelling. The One whose name is Holy dwells with the contrite. And where He dwells He makes holy.

Chapter 14

The Holy One of God

So the holy one to be born will be called the Son of God.

Luke 1:35

We believe and know that you are the Holy One of God.

John 6:69

Only once is the expression "holy one of the Lord" found in the Old Testament. It is applied to Aaron, in whom holiness, as far as it could then be revealed, had found its most complete embodiment. The title waited for its fulfillment in Him who alone, in His own person, could perfectly reveal the holiness of God on earth—Jesus the Son of the Father. In Him we see true holiness, as divine, as human, as our very own.

1. *In Him we see wherein that incomparable excellence of the divine nature consists.* "You love righteousness and hate wickedness; therefore God, your God, has set you above your companions by anointing you with the oil of joy" (Psalm 45:7). God's infinite hatred of sin and His maintenance of the right might appear to have little moral worth, as being a necessity of His nature. In the Son we see divine holiness tested. He is tried and tempted. He suffers, being tempted. He proves that holiness has indeed a moral worth: it is

ready to make any sacrifice, even to give up life and cease to be rather than consent to sin. In giving himself to die rather than yield to the temptation of sin and in giving himself to die that the Father's righteous judgment might be honored, Jesus proved that righteousness is an element of the divine holiness, and how the Holy One is sanctified in righteousness.

But this is only one side of holiness. The fire that consumes also purifies: it makes partakers of its own beautiful light-nature all that are capable of assimilation. So divine holiness not only maintains its own purity but it also communicates it. Herein was Jesus seen to be the Holy One of God: He never said, "Stand by, for I am holier than thou." His holiness proved itself to be the very incarnation of Him who had spoken, "For this is what the high and lofty One says . . . whose name is Holy; 'I live in a high and holy place, but also with him who is contrite and lowly in spirit'" (Isaiah 57:15). In Him was seen the affinity holiness has for all that are lost and helpless and sinful. He proved that holiness is not only the energy that separates itself *from* all that are impure but also in holy love separates *to* itself even the most sinful, to save and to bless. In Him we see how the divine holiness is the harmony of infinite righteousness with infinite love.

2. *Such is the divine aspect of the character of Christ as He shows in human form what God's holiness is.* But there is another aspect no less interesting and important to us. We not only want to know how God is holy but also how man must act in order to be holy as God is holy. Jesus came to teach us that it is possible to be human and yet have the life of God dwelling in us. We ordinarily think that the glory and the infinite perfection of Deity are the proper setting in which the beauty of holiness is to be seen, but Jesus proved the perfect adaptation and suitability of human nature for showing the essential glory of Deity. He showed us how—in choosing and doing

the will of God and making it His own will—man may truly be holy as God is holy.

The value of this aspect of the Incarnation depends upon our full realization of the true humanity of our Lord. Holiness, to be truly human, must not only be a gift but also an acquirement. Coming from God, it must be accepted and personally appropriated in the voluntary surrender of all that is not in accordance with it. Jesus gave up His own will and did the Father's will; this is our revelation of what human holiness is.

3. *How does it help us to have seen in Jesus that a man can be holy?* His example would only be a mockery if He could not show us the way and give us the power to become like himself. To accomplish this for us was indeed the supreme object of the Incarnation. The divine nature of Christ did not simply make *His* humanity partaker of its holiness, leaving Him still nothing more than an individual man. His divinity gave the human holiness He worked out, the holy human nature that He perfected, an infinite value and power of communication. With Him a new life, eternal life, was grafted into the stem of humanity. For all who believe in Him, He sanctified himself that they themselves might also be sanctified in truth. Because His death was the great triumph of His obedience to the will of the Father, it broke forever the dominion of sin, atoned for our guilt, and won for Him the power to make His people partakers of His own holiness. In His resurrection and ascension the power of the new life and its right to universal dominion were made manifest. He is now in truth the Holy One of God, holding in himself as head the power of a holiness at once divine and human to communicate to every member of His body.

The Holy One of God—in a fullness of meaning that is beyond our understanding, Jesus now bears this title. He is the one Holy One whom God sees, of such an infinite compass and power of holiness that He can be holiness to each of His brethren. Just as He is to God the Holy One, in whom God delights and for whose sake He delights in all who are in Christ, even so now Christ may be to us the only Holy One in whom we delight. "We believe and know that you are the Holy One of God" (John 6:69). Blessed are they who can say this and know themselves to be holy in Christ.

In speaking of the mystery of the Holy Trinity, we saw how Christ stands midway between the Father and the Spirit as the point of union in which they meet. In the Son, "the exact representation of his being" (Hebrews 1:3), we have the objective revelation of Deity, the divine holiness embodied and brought nigh. In the Holy Spirit we have the same revelation subjectively, the divine holiness entering our inmost being and revealing itself there. The work of the Holy Spirit is to reveal and glorify Christ as the Holy One of God, as He takes of His holiness and makes it ours. He shows us how all is in Christ, Christ is all for us, and we are in Christ. He shows how, as a living Savior, Christ through His Spirit takes and keeps charge of us and our life of holiness. He makes Christ indeed to be to us the Holy One of God.

Do you want to be holy? Do you want to know God's way of holiness? Learn to know Christ as the Holy One of God. In Him, you are "holy in Christ." By an act of divine power, you have been placed in Christ, and that same power keeps you there, planted and rooted in that divine fullness of life and holiness that is in Him. This holy presence and the power of His eternal life surround you. Let the Holy Spirit reveal this to you. The Holy Spirit is within you as the power of Christ and His life. Secretly, silently, but mightily, if you look to the Father for His working, He will strengthen your faith in the fact that you are in Christ, and that the divine life, which enfolds you on every side, will enter in and take possession of you. Study and pray to believe and understand that it is in Christ as the Holy One of God, in whom the holiness of God is prepared for you, that you are and may continue to abide.

Remember that Christ your Savior is the most patient and compassionate of teachers. Study holiness in the light of His countenance. He came from heaven for the very purpose of making you holy. His love and power are greater than your weakness and sinfulness. Recognize holiness as an inheritance prepared for you, as the power of a new life that Jesus waits to bestow on you. Think of it as all in Him, and of its possession as being dependent upon the possession of himself. His disciples, who hardly understood what they confessed or where they were being led, became His saints. You too will find that to love Jesus fervently and to obey Him is the sure path to holiness and the fullness of the Holy Spirit.

Most Holy Lord God! I bless you that your beloved Son, whom you sanctified and sent into this world, is now to us the Holy One of God. I ask you that my inner life may be enlightened by the Spirit so that I may by faith fully know what this means.

I want to know Him as the revelation of your holiness in human flesh, even unto death, of your infinite hatred of sin as well as your amazing love of the sinner. May my soul be filled with godly fear and yet completely trust you.

Let me know Him as the expression of your holiness in which we are to walk. And may I know Him as He worked out that holiness, communicating it to us in his human nature, making it possible for us to live a holy life.

I want to know Him as He dwells in me, the Holy One of God on the throne of my heart, breathing His Holy Spirit in me and maintaining His holy rule. So shall I live my life holy in Christ.

O my Father, it pleased you that in your Son should all fullness dwell. In Him are hidden all the treasures of wisdom and knowledge; in Him dwell the unsearchable riches of grace and holiness. I beseech you, reveal Him to me, reveal Him in me, that I may not be satisfied with thoughts and desires without the reality, but that in the power of an endless life I may know Him and be known of Him, the Holy One of God. Amen.

Personal Application

1. In the holiness of Jesus we see what ours must be: righteousness that hates sin and gives everything to see it destroyed; love that seeks the sinner and gives everything to see him saved. "Anyone who does not do what is right is not a child of God; nor is anyone who does not love his brother" (1 John 3:10).

2. It is a solemn thought that we could be studying earnestly to know what holiness is but have little of it because we have so little of Jesus. It is a blessed thought that a man may be little occupied with the thought of holiness and yet have much of it because he is full of Jesus.

3. We need all that God teaches in His Word in regard to holiness in all its aspects. We need still more to be always returning to the living center where God imparts holiness. Jesus is the Holy One of God: to have Him truly, to love Him fervently, to trust and obey Him, to be in Him—this is holiness.

4. Your holiness is treasured up in this divine, almighty, and gentle Savior—surely there need be no fear that He will not be ready or able to make you holy.

5. With such a sanctifier, how does it happen that so many seekers after holiness fail so utterly and know so little of the joy of a holy life?

6. I am sure with many it is for one reason: they seek to grasp and hold Christ in their own strength; they do not know how the Holy Spirit within reveals Jesus in their hearts.

The Holy Spirit

*By this he meant the Spirit, whom those who believed in him
were later to receive. Up to that time the Spirit had not been
given, since Jesus had not yet been glorified.*

John 7:39

*But the Counselor, the Holy Spirit, whom the Father will send in
my name, will teach you all things.*

John 14:26

*From the beginning God chose you to be saved through the
sanctifying work of the Spirit and through belief in the truth.*

2 Thessalonians 2:13

It has sometimes been said that while the holiness of God stands out
more prominently in the Old Testament, in the New it gives way to
the revelation of His love. The remark could hardly be made if it
were fully realized that the Spirit is God, and that when He uses
"Holy" as His own proper name, it is to teach us that now the holiness of God is to come nearer than ever to be clearly revealed as
the power that makes us holy. In the Holy Spirit, God the Holy One

of Israel and the Holy One of God comes close to fulfill the promise "I am the Lord that makes you holy." The unseen and unapproachable holiness of God has been revealed and brought near in the life of Christ Jesus; all that hindered our participation in it has been removed by His death. The name *Holy Spirit* teaches us that it is particularly the work of the Spirit to impart holiness to us and make it our own.

Try to realize the meaning of this: the expression that through the whole Old Testament has belonged to the Holy God is now appropriated to that Spirit that is within you. The holiness of God in Christ becomes holiness in you because His Spirit is in you. The words *Holy* and *Spirit* and the divine realities they express are now inseparably and eternally united. *You can only have as much of the Spirit as you are willing to have of holiness.* And you can only have as much holiness as you have of the indwelling Spirit.

Some pray for the Spirit because they long to have His light and joy and strength, but their prayers bring little increase of blessing or power. It is because they do not truly know or desire Him as the *Holy* Spirit. They do not know His burning purity, His searching and convicting light, His putting to death the deeds of the body, of self with its will and its power, and His leading into the fellowship of Jesus as He gave up His will and His life to the Father. The Spirit cannot work in power in them because they do not receive Him as the *Holy* Spirit, as sanctification of the Spirit. At times, such as in seasons of revival—as among the Corinthians and Galatians—He may indeed come with His gifts and mighty workings while His sanctifying power is little manifested. But unless that sanctifying power is acknowledged and accepted, His gifts will be lost. His gifts to us are only meant to prepare the way for His sanctifying power within us. We must take the lesson to heart: we can have as much of the Spirit as we are willing to have of His holiness. To be full of the Spirit means to be fully holy.

The opposite is equally true. We can have only as much holiness as we have of the Spirit. Some souls earnestly seek to be holy, but largely in their own strength. They will read books and listen carefully to sermons; they will expend great effort to grasp every thought and practice what they hear. Even so they must confess that they are still virtual strangers to the true, deep rest and joy and power of abiding in Christ and being holy in Him. They have sought for holiness more than for the Spirit. They must learn that even all the holiness that is so near and clear in Christ is beyond our reach unless the Holy Spirit dwells within and imparts it. They must learn to pray for Him and His mighty strengthening (Ephesians 3:16), to believe for Him (John 4:14; 7:37–9), in faith to yield to Him as indwelling (1 Corinthians 3:16; 6:19). They must learn to cease from self-effort in thinking and believing, in willing and in doing. They must hope in God and wait patiently for Him. By His Holy Spirit He will make us holy. To be holy means to be filled with the Spirit.

How is it that this Holy Spirit makes us holy? He reveals and imparts the holiness of Christ. Scripture tells us that Christ is made unto us sanctification. He sanctified himself for us that we ourselves might also be sanctified in truth. We have been sanctified through the offering of the body of Jesus Christ once for all. We are sanctified in Christ Jesus. The whole living Christ is a treasury of holiness for humankind. In His life on earth He exchanged the divine holiness He possessed for what was needed for this human earthly life: humility, love, and obedience to the Father. As God, He is sufficient for all that is needed for every moment in the life of every believer.

All of this is beyond our reach, except as the Holy Spirit inwardly communicates it to us. However, this is the very work for which He bears the name Holy Spirit—to glorify Jesus and to make us partakers of His holiness. He does it by unmasking the deep unholiness of our nature (Romans 7:14–23). He strengthens us to believe and receive Jesus as our life. He does it by leading us to utter despair of self, to absolute surrender of obedience to Jesus as Lord, and to the assured confidence of faith in the power of an indwelling Christ. He does it by imparting the disposition and grace of Christ in the secret depths of the heart and life, so that from the center of our being, which has been renewed and sanctified in Christ, holiness should flow out to the circumference and pervade all. Where desire has been awakened, and delight in the law of God has been created in the inner man, there—as the Spirit of this life in Christ Jesus—He sets us free from the law of sin and death in our members and leads us into the glorious liberty of the sons of God. As God within us, He communicates what God in Christ has prepared for us.

How do we obtain the working of the Holy Spirit? The answer is clear. He is the Spirit of the Holy Father and of Christ, the Holy One of God: He must be received from them. "Then the angel showed me the river of the water of life . . . flowing from the throne of God and of the Lamb" (Revelation 22:1). Jesus speaks of "the Holy Spirit, whom the Father will send in my name" (John 14:26). He taught us to ask the Father. Paul prays for the Ephesians: "I kneel before the Father . . . [that] he may strengthen you with power through his Spirit in your inner being" (Ephesians 3:14, 16). As we look to God in His holiness and all its revelation from creation on, we see how the Spirit now flows out from the throne of His holiness as the water of life. Thus our hope is awakened to believe that God will have Him work mightily in us. We then see Jesus revealing that holiness in human nature, rending the veil by His atoning death that the Spirit from the holiest of all may come forth, and as the Holy Spirit is Jesus' representative, make Him present within us. Seeing this, we become confident that faith in Jesus will bring the fullness of the Spirit.

Just as He told us to ask the Father, He told us to believe in himself. "Whoever believes in me . . . streams of living water will flow from within him" (John 7:38). Bow to the Father in the name of Christ, His Son; believe very simply in the Son as Him in whom the Father's love and blessing reach us. Then we may be assured that the Spirit, who is already within us as the Holy Spirit, will do His work in ever-increasing power. The mystery of holiness is the mystery of the Trinity: as we bow to the Father, believing in the Son, the Holy Spirit will work. Then we shall see the true meaning of what God spoke in Israel: "I am holy," thus speaks the Father; "Be holy," as my Son and in my Son; "I make holy," through the Spirit of my Son dwelling in you. Let our souls worship and cry out, "Holy, holy, holy is the Lord God of hosts."

All true knowledge and all participation in the holiness of the Father, which inspires adoration, and of the Son, which is meant to be ours—depend upon our life in the Spirit and upon our knowing and acknowledging Him as abiding in us as our life. What stands in the way of the holiness of such a Thrice-Holy God extending to more of His church and His children? The Holy Spirit is among us, is in us—it must be that we grieve and resist Him. If you would remove this hindrance, bow before the Father without delay that He may grant you the Spirit's mighty working in the inner man. Believe that the Holy Spirit, bearer to you of all the holiness of God and of Jesus, is indeed within you. Let Him take the place of self-effort. In holy silence, quiet your soul before God that He may give you wisdom. In emptiness and poverty of spirit, rest in the faith that He will work in His own way. Just as the holiness that Jesus brings is divine, so is the power by which the Holy Spirit communicates it. Yield yourself day by day in growing dependence and obedience to wait on and be led of Him. Let the fear of the Holy One rest on you. Sanctify the Lord God in your heart. Fear not only sin but self, as it boldly thrusts itself before God with its service. Let self die by refusing and denying its work. Let the Holy Spirit—in quietness and dependence, in the surrender of obedience and trust—have the rule, the free disposal of every faculty. Wait for Him—in power He will reveal and impart the holiness of the Father and the Son.

Holy, holy, holy, Lord God of hosts, the whole earth is full of your glory! Let that glory fill the heart of your child as he bows before you. I come to drink of the river of the water of life that flows from under the throne of God and of the Lamb. Glory be to God and to the Lamb for the gift that has not entered into the heart of man to conceive—the gift of the indwelling Holy Spirit.

O my Father, in the name of Jesus I ask that I may be strengthened with might by your Spirit in my inmost being. Help me to believe that you have given Him, and help me to accept and expect Him to fill and rule my whole inner being. Teach me to surrender to Him, not to will or run, not to think or work in my strength, but in quiet confidence to wait and know that He works in me. Teach me what it is to have no confidence in the flesh and to serve you in the Spirit. Teach me what it is in all things to be led by your Holy Spirit, the Spirit of your holiness.

Gracious Father, grant that through Him I may hear you speak and reveal yourself to me in power: I am holy. May He glorify Jesus to me and in me, Jesus in whom your command "Be holy" has been so blessedly fulfilled on my behalf. Let the Holy Spirit give me the anointing and the sealing that bring the perfect assurance that in Him your promise is being gloriously fulfilled: "I make you holy." Amen.

Personal Application

1. It is universally acknowledged that the Holy Spirit does not have that place of honor and power that are due Him as the revealer of the Father and the Son in the teaching of the church or the faith of believers. Seek a deep conviction that without the Holy Spirit, the clearest teaching on holiness, the most fervent desires, and even the most blessed experiences, will only be temporary, produce no permanent result, and bring no abiding rest.
2. The Holy Spirit dwells within and works in the hidden depths of

your nature. Seek above everything the clear and constant assurance that He is within you, doing His work.

3. To this end, deny self and its work in serving God. Lay down in God's presence your own power to think and pray and believe and strive—one by one, claim, accept, and believe in the hidden workings of the indwelling Spirit.

4. As the Son always spoke of the Father, so the Spirit always points to Christ. The soul that yields itself to the Spirit will learn of Him to know how Christ is our holiness, how we can always abide in Christ our sanctification. What a vain effort it is without the Spirit! "Just as [the Spirit] has taught you, remain in him" (1 John 2:27).

5. Believer, in the temple of your heart, there is a secret place within the veil where the Spirit of God dwells—often unrecognized. Bow in deep reverence before the Father and ask that He work mightily. Expect the Spirit to do His work: He will make your inner being a fit home and your heart a throne for Jesus.

Chapter 16

Holiness and Truth

Sanctify them by the truth; your word is truth.

John 17:17

*God chose you to be saved through the sanctifying work of the
Spirit and through belief in the truth.*

2 Thessalonians 2:13

The chief means of sanctification that God uses is His Word. And
yet how much reading and studying, teaching and preaching of the
Word has almost no effect in making us holy? It is not the Word
that sanctifies; God alone can sanctify. Nor is it simply through the
Word that God does it, but through the truth, which is in the Word.
As a means the Word is of unspeakable value as the vessel that con-
tains the truth—*if God uses it.* But as a means it is of no value if
God does *not* use it. Strive to connect God's Holy Word with the
holy God himself. God sanctifies in the truth through His Word.

Jesus had just said, "For I gave them the words you gave me"
(John 17:8). Do we realize what that means? Think of that great
transaction in eternity: the Infinite Being whom we call God giving
His words to His Son; in His words opening up His heart, communicating His mind and will, revealing himself and all His purpose

and love. In a divine power and reality beyond our imagination, God gave Christ His words. In the same living power Christ gave His disciples those words—full of divine life and energy to work in their hearts as they were able to receive them. Just as in the words of a man on earth we expect to find all the wisdom or all the goodness there is in him, so the word of the Thrice-Holy One is vitally alive with the holiness of God. All the holy fire—His burning zeal and His burning love—dwells in His words.

But people can be familiar with these words, study and speak them, and still be complete strangers to their holiness or their power to make holy. God himself, the Holy One, must be the one to produce holiness through the Word. Every seed in which the life of a tree is contained is encircled by a husk or shell that protects and hides the inner life. Only where the seed finds congenial soil and the husk is burst and removed can the seed germinate and grow. And only where there is a heart in harmony with God's holiness, longing for it, yielding itself to it, will the Word make one holy. The heart that is not content with the Word but seeks the living Holy One in the Word, to that heart He will reveal the truth and in it himself. It is the Word—given to us by Christ as God gave it to Him, and received by us as it was by Him to rule and fill our life—that has the power to make us holy.

But we must notice especially how our Savior says, "Sanctify them, not in the word but in the truth." Just as in man there is body, soul, and spirit, so in truth also. First there is word-truth: a man may have the correct form of words while he does not really apprehend the truth they contain. Then there is thought-truth: there may be a clear intellectual apprehension of truth without the experience of its power. The Bible speaks of truth as a living reality—this is the life-truth, in which the very Spirit of truth we profess has entered and possessed our inner being. Christ calls himself the truth: He is said to be full of grace and truth. The divine life and grace are in

Him as an actual, substantial existence and reality. He not only acts upon us by thoughts and motives but also communicates as a reality the eternal life He brought for us from the Father. The Holy Spirit is called the Spirit of truth; what He imparts is real, actual, and the very substance of unseen things. He guides into the truth, not thought-truth or doctrine only, but life-truth, the personal possession of the truth as it is in Jesus. As the Spirit of truth He is the Spirit of holiness. The life of God, which is His holiness, He brings to us as an actual possession.

It is now of this living truth, which dwells in the Word as the seed-life dwells in the husk, that Jesus says, "Sanctify them by the truth; your word is truth" (John 17:17). He would have us mark the intimate connection as well as the wide difference between the Word and the truth. The connection is one ordained by God and meant to be inseparable. "Your word is truth"; with God they are one—but not with man. There were men in close contact and continual fellowship with Jesus to whom He was only a man and nothing more. Likewise, there are Christians who know and understand the Word and yet are strangers to its true spiritual power. They have the letter but not the spirit. The truth comes to them in word but not in power. The Word does not make them holy because they do not hold it in spirit and in truth. On the contrary, there are others who receive and love the truth, who in all their dealings with the Word, yield themselves to the Spirit of truth who dwells in it and in them too. To these the Word comes as truth, as a divine reality, communicating and working that which it speaks. It is of such use of the Word that the Savior says, "Sanctify them by the truth; your word is truth." Just as the words that God gave Him were all in the power of eternal life, the love and will of God, revealing and communicating the Father's purpose, and just as God's Word was truth to Him and in Him, so it can be in us. When we thus receive it, we are made holy in the truth.

What lessons are here for the path to holiness? First, be sure that in all your contacts with God's blessed Word, you rest content with nothing short of experiencing it as the truth of God, as spirit and power. Jesus said, "If you hold to my teaching ... then you will know the truth" (John 8:31–32). No analysis can ever find or prove the life of a seed. Plant it in its proper soil and growth will testify to the life. Only as the Word of God is received in love, and as it grows and works in us, can we know its truth and be sure that it is the truth of God. As we live in the words of Jesus, in love and obedience, keeping and doing them, then the truth from heaven—the power of the divine life that there is in them—will reveal itself to us. Christ is the truth; in Him the love and grace, the very life of God, has come to earth as an existence with substance, a living, mighty power, something new that never was on earth before (John 1:17–18). Let us yield ourselves to the living Christ to possess us and to rule us as the living truth, then will God's Word be truth to us and in us.

The Spirit of Christ is the Spirit of truth. That actual heavenly reality of divine life and love in Christ, the truth, has a Spirit, who comes to communicate and impart it. Beware of trying to study or understand or even to take possession of God's Word without that Spirit through whom the Word was spoken of old. Without it we shall find only the husk. The truth or thought and sentiment may be very beautiful perhaps but have no power to make us holy. We must have the Spirit of truth within us. He will lead us into the truth; when we are in the truth, God makes us holy in it and by it. The truth must be in us and we in it. God desires truth in the inward parts. Christ says, "He who belongs to God hears what God says" (John 8:47) and "everyone on the side of truth listens to me" (John 18:37)—we must be people like this. In daily life and conduct, in thought and action, even in this lower sphere, there must be an intense love of truth and a willingness to sacrifice everything for it.

In the spiritual life there must be a deep hungering to have all our religion every day, every moment, stand fully in the truth of God. To the simple, humble, childlike spirit, the truth of the Word will be unsealed and revealed. In such the Spirit of truth comes to dwell. In such, as they daily wait before the Holy One in silence and emptiness, in reverence and holy fear, His Holy Spirit works and gives the truth within. In thus imparting Christ as revealed in the Word, in His divine life and love as their own life, He makes them holy with the holiness of Christ.

Another lesson lies in that prayer, the earthly echo of the prayer that says, "Holy Father, make them holy in the truth." Child of God, would you be holy? Cast yourself into that mighty current of intercession ever flowing into and ever reaching the Father's bosom. Be borne upon it until your whole soul cries with unutterable groanings too deep and too intense for human speech, "Holy Father, sanctify me holy by the truth." Then trusting in Christ as the truth and reality of what you desire and trusting in His all-prevailing intercession as you wait for the Spirit within as the Spirit of truth, look up to the Father—expect His own direct and almighty working to make you holy. The mystery of holiness is the mystery of the Triune One. The deeper entrance into the holy life rests in the fellowship of the Trinity. It is the Father who establishes us in Christ, who gives each day anew of the Holy Spirit. To the Holy Father the soul must look up continually in the prayer "Sanctify me holy by the truth."

In the word *holy* we have the central thought of the high-priestly prayer. As the Father's attribute (John 17:11), as the Son's work for himself and us (v. 19), as the direct work of the Father through the Spirit (vv. 17, 20)—all reveal the glory of God in himself and in us. Let us enter into the holiest of all and bow with our great High Priest. Then let the deep, unceasing cry go up for all the church of God, "Holy Father, sanctify them holy by the truth: your word is truth!" The word in which God makes holy is summed up in this: *Holy in Christ.* May God make it truth to us!

Blessed Father, you told Israel, "I the Lord am holy and make holy." But it is only in your beloved Son that the full glory of your holiness, making us holy, has been revealed.

We thank you that your Son has given us the words you gave Him, and that as He received them from you in life and power, we may receive them too. O Father! With our whole heart we do receive them. Let the Spirit make them truth and life within us. So shall we know you as the Holy One, consuming the sin, renewing the sinner.

We bless you most of all for your blessed Son, the Holy One of God, the living Word in whom the truth dwells. We thank you that in His never-ceasing intercession, this cry reaches you, "Father, sanctify them in your truth." We praise you that the answer ever streams forth from your glory. Holy Father, make us holy in your truth, in your wonderful revelation of yourself in Him who is the truth. Let your Holy Spirit have dominion in our hearts so that by Jesus' sanctifying himself for us, we may be sanctified in the truth. May He be to us the way, the truth, and the life. Amen.

Personal Application

1. God is the God of truth—not truth in speaking only or truth of doctrine—but truth of existence, or life in its divine reality. And Christ is the truth; the actual embodiment of this divine life. There is a kingdom of truth, of divine spiritual realities, of which Christ is King. And the very essence of all this truth of God in Christ is the Spirit. He is the Spirit of truth. He leads us into it, so that we are of the truth and walk in it. The reality there is in God. Holiness is the deepest root of the truth; the Spirit of truth is the Holy Spirit.

2. It is the work of the Father to make us holy in the truth. Let us bow very low in childlike trust as we pray, "Holy Father, make us holy in the truth." He will do it.

3. It is the intercession of the Son that asks and obtains this bless-

ing. Let us take our place in Him and rejoice in the assurance of an answer.

4. It is the Spirit of truth through whom the Father does this work, so that we may dwell in the truth and the truth in us. Let us yield freely and fully to the leading of the Spirit, in our dealing with God's Word, so that as the Son prays, the Father may make us holy in the truth.

5. In the light of the Three in One, let us never read the Word except with this aim: to be made holy in the truth by God.

Chapter 17

Holiness and Crucifixion

For them I sanctify myself, that they too may be truly sanctified.

John 17:19

Then he said, "Here I am, I have come to do your will.". . . And by that will, we have been made holy through the sacrifice of the body of Jesus Christ once for all. . . . because by one sacrifice he has made perfect forever those who are being made holy.

Hebrews 10:9–10, 14

In His high-priestly prayer on His way to Gethsemane and Calvary, Jesus said to the Father, "I sanctify myself." Not long before He had spoken of himself as "the one whom the Father set apart as his very own and sent into the world" (John 10:36). From Scripture we are familiar with the thought that what God has sanctified man must sanctify. The work of the Father in sanctifying the Son is the basis and groundwork of the work of the Son in sanctifying himself. If His holiness as man was to be a free and personal possession, accepted and assimilated in voluntary and conscious self-determination, it was not enough that the Father sanctify Him; He must sanctify himself too.

This self-sanctifying of our Lord took place through His whole life but culminates and comes out with special clarity in His crucifixion. Wherein it consists is explained in Hebrews. The Messiah said, "Here I am, I have come to do your will." And then it is added, "By that will, we have been made holy through the sacrifice of the body of Jesus Christ." It was the offering of the body of Christ that was the will of God; in doing that will He sanctified us. About the doing of His Father's will in the offering of His body He said, "I sanctify myself, that they too may be truly sanctified." Giving up His will to God's will in the agony of Gethsemane, and then doing that will in obedience unto death, Christ sanctified himself and us.

The holiness of God is revealed in His will. Holiness even in the Divine Being has no moral value except as it is freely willed. In speaking of the Trinity, theologians have pointed out how, as the Father represents the absolute necessity of everlasting goodness, the Son proves its liberty: within the Divine Being it is willed in love. And this was the work of the Son on earth, amid the trials and temptations of a human life to accept and hold fast at any sacrifice, and with His whole heart to will the will of the Father.

"Although he was a son, he learned obedience from what he suffered" (Hebrews 5:8). In Gethsemane the conflict between the will of human nature and the divine will reached its height—it manifests itself in language that has us in awe of His sinlessness as He speaks of His will in antithesis to God's will. But the struggle is a victory because, clearly conscious of what it would mean to have His own will, He surrenders it and says, "May your will be done" (Matthew 26:42). To enter into the will of God He gives up His life. In His crucifixion He reveals the law of sanctification. Holiness is the full entrance of our will into God's will. Put simply, holiness is the entrance of God's will at the cost of our will. The only end of our will and deliverance from it is death to it under the righteous judgment of God. In the surrender to the death of the cross, Christ sanctified himself, and us, that we also might be sanctified in truth.

Now, just as the Father sanctified Him, and He in virtue thereof appropriated it and sanctified himself, so we, whom He has sanctified, have to appropriate it for ourselves. In no other way than crucifixion, the giving up of himself to death, could Christ realize the sanctification He had from the Father. And in no other way can we realize the sanctification we have in Him. His and our sanctification bear the common stamp of the cross.

We have seen before that obedience is the path to holiness. In Christ we see that the path to perfect holiness is perfect obedience. That means obedience unto death, even the death of the cross. The sanctification that Christ wrought for us, offering His body, bears the death mark, and we cannot partake of it either except as we die to self and its will. Crucifixion is the path to sanctification.

This lesson is in harmony with all we have seen. The first revelation of God's holiness to Moses was accompanied by the command "Put off." God's praise, as glorious in holiness, fearful in praises, was spoken over the dead bodies of the Egyptians. When Moses on Sinai was commanded to sanctify the Mount, it was said, "There shall not a hand touch it; whether it be beast or man, it shall not live." *The holiness of God is death to all that is in contact with sin.* Only through death, through the shedding of blood, was there access to the holiest of all. Christ chose death, even death as a curse, that He might sanctify himself for us, and open to us the path to holiness, to the holiest of all, to the Holy One. It is still the same today.

No man can see God and live. Only in death, the death of self and of nature, can we draw near and behold God. Christ led the way. No man can see God and live. "Then let me die, Lord," one has cried, "but see Thee I must!" So real is this right that Christ gives us and so genuine our union to Him that we may live in His death; as self is kept in the place of death day by day, the life and the holiness of Christ can be ours.

Where is the place of death? How can the crucifixion that leads to holiness and to God be accomplished in us? Thank God! It is through no work of our own, no weary process of self-crucifixion. The crucifixion that is to sanctify us is an accomplished fact. The cross bears the banner "It is finished" (John 19:30). On it Christ sanctified himself for us that we might be sanctified in truth. Our crucifixion, like our sanctification, is something that in Christ has been completely and perfectly finished. "And by that will we have been made holy through the sacrifice of the body of Jesus Christ once for all" (Hebrews 10:10). "By one sacrifice he has made perfect forever those who are being made holy" (Hebrews 10:14). In that fullness, which it is the Father's good pleasure should dwell in Christ, the crucifixion of our old man, of the flesh, of the world, of ourselves, is all a spiritual reality. He who desires and knows and accepts Christ fully receives all this in Him.

Christ had previously been known especially for His pardoning, quickening, and saving grace. Now as He is sought again in the role of a real deliverer from the power of sin—as a sanctifier—He comes and includes the soul in the fellowship of the sacrifice of His will. "He [did] away with sin by the sacrifice of himself" (Hebrews 9:26) must become true of us as it is of Him. He reveals how it is part of His salvation to make us partakers of a will entirely surrendered to the will of God, of a life that had yielded itself to death and then had been given back from the dead by the power of God—a life of which the crucifixion of self-will was the spirit and the power. He reveals this. The soul that sees and consents to it, that yields its will and its life and believes in Jesus as its death and life, and in His crucifixion as its possession and its inheritance, enters into the enjoyment and experience of it—*now*. "I died . . . that I might live for God. I have been crucified with Christ and I no longer live, but Christ lives in me" (Galatians 2:19–20). The life it now lives is by faith in the Son of God, the daily acceptance in faith of Him who lives within us in the power of a death that has been passed through and forever finished.

"For them I sanctify myself, that they too may be truly sanctified" (John 17:19). "I have come to do your will. . . . And by that will," the will of God accomplished by Christ, "we have been made holy through the sacrifice of the body of Jesus Christ" (Hebrews 10:9–10). Christ gave up His will in Gethsemane and accepted God's will by dying. By this obedience He sanctified himself. The death to self, the utter, absolute giving up of our own life with its will and power and aims to the cross, the daily bearing of that cross—not one on which we are yet to be crucified, but the cross of Christ— this is the secret of the life of holiness; this is true sanctification.

Is this the holiness that you are seeking? Do you see that God alone is holy, that we are unholy, and that there is no way for us to be made holy except by our being crucified with Christ? "We always carry around in our body the death of Jesus, so that the life of Jesus may also be revealed in our body" (2 Corinthians 4:10). This is the pathway for all who truly seek to be sanctified.

Jesus sanctified himself for us that we also might be sanctified in truth. The secret roots of our being are planted in Jesus. Deeper down than we can see or feel is our Vine, bearing and quickening us. In a way and to a degree far beyond our comprehension, intensely divine and real, we are in Him who sanctified himself for us. Let us remain where God has placed us. Let us pray to the Father to strengthen us by His Spirit that Christ as our sanctification may dwell in our hearts, that the power of His death and His life may be revealed in us, and God's will be done in us as it was in Him.

Holy Father! I bless you for this word and the work of your beloved Son. In His never-ceasing intercession you always hear the prayer "For them I sanctify myself, that they too may be truly sanctified."

Strengthen me by your Spirit so that by faith I may accept and live the holiness prepared for me in my Lord Jesus. Give me spiritual understanding to know what it means that as by faith I abide in Him, its power will cover my whole life. Let His surrender to your will, His continual dependence and obedience, be its root and strength, His death to the world and to sin be its daily rule. Above all let the living Jesus, who was sanctified for me, be my only hope and trust. How shall I bless and love and glorify you for this wondrous grace! You gave yourself that I might be made holy in you. I give myself to you with thanks and praise. Amen.

Personal Application

1. "If anyone would come after me, he must deny himself and take up his cross and follow me" (Matthew 16:24; Mark 8:34; Luke 9:23). Jesus means that our life shall be the exact counterpart of His, including His crucifixion. The beginning of such a life is the denial of self, to give Christ His rightful place. The Jews would not deny self, but "disowned the Holy and Righteous One. . . . You killed the author of life" (Acts 3:14–15). The choice is still between Christ and self.

2. The steps in this path are these: First, the deliberate decision that self will be given over to death; then the surrender to Christ crucified to make us partakers of His crucifixion: "For we know that our old self was crucified" (Romans 6:6); the faith that says, "I have been crucified with Christ" (Galatians 2:20); and finally, the power to live as a crucified one, to glory in the cross of Christ.

3. This is God's way of holiness, a divine mystery, which the Holy Spirit alone can daily maintain in us. Blessed be God, it is the life that a Christian can live because Christ lives in us.

4. The central thought is: We are in Christ, who gave up His will and did the will of God. By the Holy Spirit the mind that was in Him is in us, the will of self is crucified, and we live in the will of God.

Chapter 18

Holiness and Faith

That they may receive forgiveness of sins and a place among
those who are sanctified by faith in me.

Acts 26:18

The more we study Scripture in the light of the Holy Spirit or practice the Christian life in His power, the deeper becomes our conviction of the unique and central place faith has in God's plan of salvation. We see, too, that it is fitting and right that it should be so:
the very nature of things demands it. Because God is a spiritual and
invisible being, every revelation of Him, whether in His works, His
Word, or His Son, calls for faith. Faith is the spiritual sense of the
soul, being to it what the senses are to the body. By faith alone we
enter into communication and contact with God.

Faith is that meekness of soul that waits in stillness to hear, understand, and accept what God says, and to receive, retain, and possess what God gives or does. By faith we allow, we welcome God
himself, the living person, to enter in to make His abode with us
and become our very life. However well we think we know it, we
always have to learn the truth afresh, to see a deeper and fuller application of it, that in the Christian life faith is the first thing—the
one thing—that pleases God and brings blessing to us. And because

holiness is God's highest glory and the highest blessing He has for us, it is especially in the life of holiness that we need to live by faith alone.

Our Lord speaks here of "those who are sanctified by faith in me." He himself is our sanctification as He is our justification: for both it is faith that God asks, and both are equally given at once. The participle used here is not the present, denoting a process or work that is being carried on, but the aorist, indicating an act done once for all. When we believe in Christ, we receive the whole Christ, our justification and our sanctification: we are all at once accepted by God as righteous and holy in Him. God counts and calls us what we really are—sanctified ones in Christ. As we are led to see what God sees and as our faith grasps that the holy life of Christ is ours in actual possession, to be accepted and appropriated for daily use, then we shall really be able to live the life God calls us to—the life of holy ones in Christ Jesus. We shall then be in the right position in which what is called our progressive sanctification can be worked out. It will be the acceptance and application in daily life of the power of a holy life that has been prepared in Jesus, which has in the union with Him become our present and permanent possession and that works in us according to the measure of our faith.

From this point of view it is evident that faith has a twofold operation. Faith is the evidence of things not seen, though now actually existing, the substance of things hoped for, but not yet present. It deals with the unseen present as well as with the unseen future. As the evidence of things not seen, it rejoices in Christ our complete sanctification as a present possession. Through faith I simply look to what Christ is as revealed in the Word by the Holy Spirit. Claiming all He is as my own, I know that His holiness, His holy nature and life are mine; I am a holy one. By faith in Him I have been sanctified.

This is the first aspect of sanctification: it looks to what is a complete and finished work, an absolute reality. As the substance of things hoped for, this faith reaches out in the assurance of hope to the future, to things I do not yet see or experience, and claims day by day, out of Christ our sanctification, what it needs for practical holiness: "to be holy in all manner of living."

This is the second aspect of sanctification: in personal experience I depend upon Jesus to supply, gradually and unceasingly, for the need of each moment, all that has been treasured up in His fullness. "You are in Christ Jesus, who has become for us . . . from God . . . holiness" (1 Corinthians 1:30).

Under its first aspect faith says, "I know I am in Him, and all His holiness is mine." In its second aspect it says, "I trust in Him for the grace and the strength I need each moment to live a holy life."

And yet it need hardly be said these two are one. It is one Jesus who is our sanctification, whether we look at it in the light of what He is made for us once for all, or what, as the fruit of that, He becomes to our experience day by day. It is one faith. The more we rejoice in Jesus our sanctification, the bolder we are to expect the fulfillment of every promise for daily life and the stronger to claim the victory over every sin. Faith in Jesus is the secret of a holy life. All holy conduct, all holy deeds, are the fruit of faith in Jesus as our holiness.

We know how faith acts and what its great hindrances are in the matter of justification. It is well that we remind ourselves that there are the same dangers in the exercise of sanctifying as of justifying faith. Faith in God stands opposed to trust in self: especially to the willing and working of self. Faith is hindered by every effort to do something ourselves. Faith looks to God working and yields itself to His strength, as revealed in Christ through the Spirit. It allows God to work both to will and to do. Faith must work, that is, manifest itself. Without works it is dead; by works it is made known. In Jesus

Christ, as Paul says, nothing avails but "faith working by love." But these works, which faith in God's working inspires and performs, are very different from the works in which a believer often puts forth his best efforts, only to find that he fails. The true life of holiness, the life of those who are sanctified in Christ, has its root and its strength in an abiding sense of utter impotence, in the deep restfulness that trusts in the working of a divine power and life, in the entire personal surrender to the loving Savior in that faith that consents to be nothing that He may be all.

It may appear impossible to discern or describe the difference between the working of self and the working of Christ through faith: but if we know there is such a difference, and we learn to distrust our flesh and count on Christ's working, the Holy Spirit will lead us. Faith's works are Christ's works.

Just as faith is hindered by effort, so faith also is hindered by the desire to see and feel. If you believe, you will see (John 1:50–51). The Holy Spirit will seal our faith with a divine experience; we shall see the glory of God. But this is His work. Ours is when all appears dark and cold, in the face of all that nature or experience testifies, and we still believe in Jesus as our all-sufficiency, in whom we are perfected before God. Complaints as to lack of feeling, weakness, or deadness seldom profit. The soul that refuses to be preoccupied with itself, either with its own weakness or the strength of the Enemy, but who looks to what Jesus is and has promised to do—to that soul progress in holiness will be a joyful march from victory to victory. "The Lord himself will fight for you." This thought, so often repeated in connection with Israel's possession of the Promised Land, is the food of faith. In conscious weakness, in the presence of its enemies, it sings the conqueror's song. When God appears not to be doing what we trusted Him for, then is the time for faith to glory in Him.

Perhaps nothing more fully reveals the true character of faith than joy and praise. You promise a child a present tomorrow and at once he says, "Thank you," and is glad. Joyful thanks are the proof that your promise was believed. You may be told by a friend of a rich legacy he is leaving you in his will. It may not come true for years, but even now it makes you glad. We have already seen what an element of holiness joy is; it is especially an element of holiness by faith. God's provision by which my holiness is in Jesus and I may allow Him to work in me is beautiful and perfect. Each time I realize the truth of this, my heart ought to rise up in praise and thanks. Instead of thinking that this life of holiness by faith is a life of difficult attainment and continual self-denial, we ought to praise God that He has made it possible and sure for us. We can be holy because Jesus the loving One is our holiness. Praise will express our faith; praise will prove it; praise will strengthen it. "Then believed they his words; they sang his praise." Praise will commit us to faith: we shall see that we have only one thing to do—to go on in a faith that always trusts and praises. It is in a living, loving attachment to Jesus that rejoices in Him and praises Him continually for what He is to us that faith proves itself and receives the power of holiness.

"Sanctified by faith in me." It is the personal, living Jesus who offers himself in all the riches of His power and love as the object, the strength, the life of our faith. He tells us that if we would be always and in everything holy, we must see to only one thing: to be always and altogether full of faith in Him. Faith is the eye of the soul, the power by which we discern the presence of the Unseen One as He comes to give himself to us. Faith not only sees but appropriates and assimilates. Let the Holy Spirit who dwells in us do that for which He has been given to us: to quicken and strengthen our faith. Faith is surrender, yielding ourselves to Jesus to allow Him to do His work in us, submitting ourselves to Him to live out His life and work out His will in us. Thus we shall find Him giving himself entirely to us and taking complete possession. So faith will be power, the power of obedience to do God's will. This is "our most holy faith, the faith delivered to the holy ones." To the single-hearted, the secret of holiness is simple: Jesus. We are in Him, our sanctification. He personally is our holiness, and the life of faith in Him that receives and possesses Him must necessarily be a life of holiness. Jesus says we are "sanctified by faith in [him]."

Beloved Lord, again I have seen with adoring wonder what you are willing to be to me. It is in you and a life of living fellowship with you that I am to become holy. In the simple life of personal attachment, of trust and love, of surrender and consecration, you will become my all and make me a partaker of you and of your holiness.

Blessed Lord Jesus, I do believe in you—help my unbelief. I confess what still remains of unbelief and count on your presence to conquer and cast it out. My soul sees more and more how you alone are my life and my holiness. You enlarge my heart to rejoice in you as my all and assure me that you take possession and fill the temple of my being with your glory. You are teaching me that however weak and human and disappointing experiences may be, your Holy Spirit is the strength of my faith, leading me into a stronger and deeper confidence in you.

I take your Word today, "Sanctified by faith in me," as a new revelation of your love and its purpose in me. In you alone is the power of my holiness; in you is the power of my faith. Blessed be your name for giving me a place among those who believe your Word. Amen.

Personal Application

1. Let us remember that it is a living faith that has the power to sanctify. Anyone who casts his soul wholly on Jesus, who calls forth simple trust, whether it is in the trial of faith or the work of faith, is helped toward holiness because it brings him into living contact with the Holy One.
2. It is only through the Holy Spirit that Christ and His holiness are

day by day revealed and made ours by actual possession. And so the faith that receives Him is of the Spirit too. Yield yourself in simplicity and trust to His working. Do not be afraid, as if you cannot believe. You have the Spirit of faith within you; you have the power to believe. And you may ask God to strengthen you by His Spirit in the inner man for the faith that receives Christ and the indwelling that knows no lack.

3. I have only as much faith as I have of the Spirit. This then is what I most need: to live entirely under the influence of the Spirit.

4. Just as the eye is receptive and yields to allow the object placed before it to make its impression, so faith allows the impression of God to be made on the soul when He draws nigh. Was not the faith of Abraham the fruit of God's drawing near and speaking to him, making an impression of God on him? Let us gaze on the divine mystery of Christ our holiness: His presence, waited for and welcomed, will work out our faith.

> Holiness by faith in Jesus,
> not the effort of thine own;
> Sin's dominion crushed and broken
> by the power of grace alone.
> God's own holiness within thee,
> His own beauty on thy brow—
> This shall be thy pilgrim brightness,
> this thy blessed portion now.
>
> —Frances Ridley Havergal

Chapter 19

Holiness and Resurrection

*Regarding his Son, who as to his human nature was a
descendant of David, and who through the Spirit of holiness was
declared with power to be the Son of God by his resurrection
from the dead: Jesus Christ our Lord.*

Romans 1:3–4

These words speak of a twofold birth of Christ. According to the flesh, He was born of the seed of David. According to the Spirit, He was the first begotten from the dead. Just as He was a son of David by virtue of His birth through the flesh, so He was declared to be the Son of God with power in virtue of His birth by the Resurrection. The life He received through His first birth was a life in and after the flesh with its weaknesses, but the new life He received in the Resurrection was a life in the power of the Spirit of holiness.

The expression "the Spirit of holiness" is a peculiar one. Here the word used for God's holiness is not the same word as that used in Hebrews 12:10, which describes holiness in the abstract as the attribute of an object, but another word (also used in 2 Corinthians 7:1 and 1 Thessalonians 3:13) expressing the habit of holiness in its actions—practical holiness or sanctity. Paul used this word because He wished to emphasize the thought that Christ's resurrection was definitely the result of that life of holiness and self-sanctifying that culminated in His death. It was the Spirit of holiness by which He lived and the power by which He was raised again. He teaches us that life and death of self-sanctification, in which alone our sanctification stands, was the root and ground of His resurrection and of its declaration that He was the Son of God with power, the first begotten from the dead. The Resurrection was the fruit of His life of holiness.

And so the life of holiness becomes the property of all who are partakers of the Resurrection. The resurrection life and the Spirit of holiness are inseparable. Christ sanctified himself in death that we ourselves might be sanctified in truth: when in virtue of the Spirit of sanctification He was raised from the dead, that Spirit of holiness proved to be the power of the resurrection life.

As a believer you have a part in this new life. You have been given a "new birth into a living hope through the resurrection of Jesus Christ from the dead" (1 Peter 1:3). You "have been raised with Christ" (Colossians 3:1). You are commanded to "count yourselves . . . alive to God in Christ Jesus" (Romans 6:11). But this life can work in power only as you seek to know it, to yield to it, and to let it have full possession of you. If you do this, one of the most important things to see is that just as it was by virtue of the Spirit of holiness that Christ was raised, so also the Spirit of that same holiness must be in you the mark and the power of your life. Study to know and possess the Spirit of holiness as it was seen in the life of your Lord.

What was the secret of that holiness? The key lies here: "Here I am . . . I have come to do your will, O God" (Hebrews 10:7). "And by that will," as done by Christ, "we have been made holy through the sacrifice of the body of Jesus Christ once for all" (Hebrews 10:10). This was Christ's sanctifying himself in life and in death. This was what the Spirit of holiness worked in Him. This is what the same Spirit, the Spirit of life in Christ Jesus, will work in us: a life in the will of God is a life of holiness. Realize that Christ came to reveal what true holiness could be under the conditions of human life and weakness. He came to work it out for you so that He might communicate it to you by His Spirit. Unless you understand and fully accept it, the Spirit cannot make you holy. With your whole heart try to grasp this truth: The will of God accepted without condition is the power of holiness.

Any attempt to be holy as Christ is holy, with and in His holiness, must start here. Many seek to take parts of the life or image of Christ and try to imitate it, and yet completely fail in other points. They have not seen that Jesus calls us to deny self in the full meaning of that word. In not one single thing is our own will to be done: Jesus, who only did the Father's will, must rule our lives in every aspect. To "stand firm in all the will of God" must be the purpose, the prayer, the expectation of the disciple. Contrary to what we may fear, it is possible to know the will of the Father in everything. "If anyone chooses to do God's will, he will find out whether my teaching comes from God or whether I speak on my own" (John 7:17). The Father will not keep the willing child in ignorance of His will. As surrender to the Spirit of holiness, to Jesus and the dominion of His holy life, becomes more natural and complete, sin and self-will will be discovered, the spiritual understanding will be increased, and the law written in the heart will become intelligible. Neither do we need to fear that it will be impossible to do the will of the Father when it becomes known. When the grief of failure and sin has driven the believer into the experience of Romans 7: "In my inner being I delight in God's law" (v. 22) and the cry "What a wretched man I am!" (v. 24)—deliverance will come. The Spirit works not only to will but also to do. Where the believer could only complain "I have the desire to do what is good, but I cannot carry it out" (Romans 7:18), now the Spirit gives the strength to say, "through

Christ Jesus the law of the Spirit of life set me free from the law of sin and death" (Romans 8:2).

In this faith—that it is possible to know and do the will of God in all things—take from Him your life principle: "I have come to do your will" (Hebrews 10:9). It is the principle of the resurrection life. Without it Jesus would never have been raised again. It is the principle of the new life in you. Accept it. Realize it. Act upon it. Many a believer has found that a few simple words of dedication, expressive of the purpose to do God's will in everything, have been an entrance into the joy and power of the resurrection life previously unknown. The will of God is the complete expression of His moral perfection, His divine holiness. To take one's place in the center of that will, to live it out, to be borne and sustained by it—all these were the power of that life of Jesus that could not be held by death, could not help but burst forth in resurrection glory. What it was to Jesus it will be to us.

Holiness is life: this is the simplest expression of the truth our text teaches. There can be no holiness until a new life has been implanted. The new life cannot grow and experience resurrection power, cannot bring forth fruit, except by growing in holiness. As long as the believer is living the mixed life, part in the flesh and part in the spirit, with some of self and some of Christ, he seeks in vain for holiness. It is the new life that is the holy life: the full apprehension of it in faith and the full surrender to it in conduct will be the highway of holiness. Jesus lived and died and rose again to prepare for us a new nature, to be received day by day in the obedience of faith. We "have put on the new self, which is being renewed in knowledge in the image of its Creator" (Colossians 3:10). Let the inner life, hidden with Christ in God, and also hidden deep within the recesses of our inmost being, be acknowledged, waited on, yielded to. It will work itself out in all the beauty of holiness.

Further, this life is not like the life of nature, involuntarily working toward its object in obedience to the law of its being. This life is the Spirit of life in Christ Jesus—the Spirit of holiness—the Holy Spirit dwelling in us as a divine person, entering into fellowship with us and leading us into the fellowship of the living Christ. It is this that fills our life with hope and joy. The risen Savior breathed the Holy Spirit on His disciples: the Spirit brings Him into our hearts as a personal friend, a living guide and helper. The Spirit of holiness is the presence and the power of the living Christ. Jesus said of the Spirit, "You know him" (John 14:17). It is our greatest need to know the Holy Spirit, the Spirit of Christ. How else can we "walk after the Spirit" and follow His leading if we do not know Him or His voice or His way?

It is from the grave of the flesh and the will of self that the Spirit of holiness breaks out in resurrection power. We must accept death to the flesh and death to self with its willing and working as the birthplace of our experience of the power of the Spirit of holiness. In each struggle with sin, in each exercise of faith or prayer, we must enter into the death of Jesus and death to self. Because "we are [not] competent in ourselves to claim anything for ourselves" (2 Corinthians 3:5) we must in quiet faith expect the Spirit of Christ to do His work. The Spirit will work, strengthening you mightily in the inner man and building up within you a holy temple for the Lord. And the time will come (if not yet, soon) when the conscious indwelling of Christ in your heart by faith, the full revelation and enthronement of Him as ruler and keeper of your heart and life, will become a personal experience. It is according to the Spirit of holiness, by the resurrection from the dead, that the Son of God will be declared with power in the kingdom that is within you.

Most Holy Lord God, we do bless you that you raised your Son from the dead and gave Him glory that our faith and hope might be in you. You made His resurrection the power of eternal life in us, and now, just as He was raised, so we may walk in newness of life. As the Spirit of holiness dwelt and worked in Him, it dwells and works in us and becomes in us the Spirit of life.

O God, we beseech you to perfect your work in your saints. Give them a deeper sense of the holy calling with which you have called them in Christ. Help all to accept the Spirit of His life on earth and delight in the will of God as the spirit of their life. May those who have never yet fully accepted this be brought to do it, and in faith in the power of the new life to say, "I accept the will of God as my only law." May the Spirit of holiness be the spirit of their lives!

Father, we ask, let Christ in an ever-increasing experience of His resurrection power be revealed in our hearts as the Son of God, Lord and Ruler within us. Let His life within renew our outer life, so that in the home and in society, in thought and speech and action, in faith practice and in business, His life may shine from us in the beauty of holiness. Amen.

Personal Application

1. Scripture regards the Resurrection in two different aspects. In one view, it is the title to the new life, the source of our justification (Romans 4:25; 1 Corinthians 15:17). In another, it is our regeneration, the power of the new life working in us, the source of our sanctification (Romans 6:4; 1 Peter 1:3). Pardon and holiness are inseparable; they have the same source—union with the risen, living Christ.

2. The blessedness to the disciples of having a risen Christ was this: He whom they thought dead came and revealed himself to them. Christ lives to reveal himself to you and to me; wait on Him, trust Him for this. He will reveal himself to you as your sanctification. See to it that you have Him in living possession, that you have His holiness.

3. The life of Christ is the holiness of Christ. The reason we so often

fail in the pursuit of holiness is that the old life, the flesh, in its own strength seeks for holiness as a beautiful garment to wear and enter heaven with. It is the daily death to self out of which the life of Christ rises.

4. To die, to live in Christ, to be holy—how can we attain it? It all comes "through the Spirit." Have the Holy Spirit within you. Say daily, "I believe in the Holy Spirit and His work in me."

5. When Christ lives in us and His mind (as it found expression in His words and work on earth) enters and fills our will and personal consciousness, then our union with Him becomes what He meant it to be. It is the Spirit of His holy conduct that must be in us.

Chapter 20

Holiness and Liberty

You have been set free from sin and have become slaves to righteousness. . . . Just as you used to offer the parts of your body in slavery to impurity and to ever-increasing wickedness, so now offer them in slavery to righteousness leading to holiness. . . . Now that you have been set free from sin and have become slaves to God, the benefit you reap leads to holiness, and the result is eternal life.

Romans 6:18–19, 22

This matter arose because some false brothers had infiltrated our ranks to spy on the freedom we have in Christ Jesus and to make us slaves.

Galatians 2:4

It is for freedom that Christ has set us free. Stand firm, then, and do not let yourselves be burdened again by a yoke of slavery.

Galatians 5:1

No possession is more precious or priceless than liberty. Nothing is more inspiring and elevating. On the other hand, nothing is more depressing and degrading than slavery. It robs a man of what constitutes his manhood, the power of self-decision, self-action, of being and doing what he would.

Sin is slavery—the bondage to a foreign power that has obtained control over us and often compels a most reluctant service. The redemption of Christ restores our liberty and sets us free from the power of sin. If we are truly to live as redeemed ones, we need not only to look at the work Christ did to accomplish our redemption but also to accept and comprehend how complete, how sure, how absolute the liberty is with which He has made us free. It is only as we stand firm in the freedom we have in Christ Jesus that we can have our fruit unto sanctification.

It is remarkable how seldom the word *holiness* occurs in the great argument of Romans and how, where it is used in chapter 6 with the expression "slaves to God," it is distinctly set forth as the aim and fruit to be reached through a life of righteousness (vv. 15–23). It teaches us that liberty from the power of sin and surrender to the service of righteousness are not of themselves holiness, but are the sure and only path by which they can be reached. A true insight and a full entering into our freedom in Christ are indispensable to a life of holiness. It was when Israel was freed from Pharaoh that God began to reveal himself as the Holy One; it is as we know ourselves "freed from sin," delivered from the hand of all our enemies, that we shall serve God in righteousness and holiness all the days of our life.

To understand correctly "being made free from sin," we must beware of a twofold error: We must neither narrow it down to less than it is nor put more into it than the Holy Spirit intends. Paul is speaking neither of an imputation nor an experience. We must not limit the meaning to being free from the curse or punishment of sin. The context shows that he is speaking not of our judicial standing but of a spiritual reality—our being in living union with Christ in His death and resurrection, and so being completely removed from the dominion or power of sin. "Sin shall not be your master" (Romans 6:14). Neither is he as yet speaking of an experience where we feel that we are free from all sin. He speaks of the great fact of Christ's having delivered us from the power that sin had to compel us to do its will and its work. He urges us in the faith of this glorious fact, boldly to refuse to listen to the temptation to sin. To know our liberty that we have in Christ, our freedom from sin's mastery and power, is the way to realize it as an experience.

In past times when Turks or Moors made slaves of Christians, large sums were frequently paid to ransom those who were in bondage. But it happened more than once that the ransomed ones, far in the interior of the slave country, never received the news; the masters were only too glad to keep it from them. Others received the word, but had grown too accustomed to their bondage to stir themselves to try to reach the coast and freedom. Slothfulness or hopelessness kept them in slavery. They could not believe that they would ever be able to reach the land of liberty in safety. The ransom had been paid. In truth, they were free; but by reason of ignorance or lack of courage, in actuality they remained in bondage. Christ's redemption has so completely made an end of sin and the legal power it had over us—for "the power of sin is the law" (1 Corinthians 15:56)—that in the deepest reality sin has no power to compel our obedience. Only as we allow it to reign again and yield ourselves as its servants can it exercise dominion over us. Satan does his utmost to keep believers in ignorance of this completeness of their freedom from his slavery. Believers are limited in their own thoughts as to what redemption means, and weak in their desire and prayers to see and possess its fullness of deliverance and blessing. Because of this, the experience of the extent to which the freedom from sin can be realized is weak compared to all that is available. "Where the Spirit of the Lord is there is freedom." This liberty becomes ours when by the Holy Spirit with His light and leading within we humbly watch for it and yield to it.

In the sixth chapter of Romans Paul speaks of freedom from sin, and in chapter seven (vv. 3, 4, 6) of freedom from the law; both are privileges that are ours by being in Christ and in union with Him. In chapter eight (v. 2) he speaks of this freedom as having become ours by experience. He says, "The law of the Spirit of life set me free from the law of sin and death." The freedom that is ours in Christ must become ours in personal appropriation and enjoyment through the Holy Spirit. The latter depends on the former: the fuller the faith, the clearer the insight; the more triumphant the glorying in Christ Jesus and the liberty with which He has made us free, the speedier and the fuller the entrance into the glorious liberty of the children of God. Just as the liberty is in Christ alone, so the Spirit of Christ alone makes it ours in practical possession. "The Spirit of life set me free from the law of sin and death. Where the Spirit of the Lord is, there is freedom." The Spirit reveals Jesus to us as Lord and Master, the new Master, who alone has authority over us. He leads us to yield ourselves, to present our members, to surrender our whole life to the service of God in Christ. As He does this, our faith in freedom from sin becomes a realization. Believing in the completeness of redemption, the captive goes forth as "the Lord's freedman." He knows that sin no longer has power for one moment to command obedience. It may seek to assert its old right, it may speak in the tone of authority, it may frighten into fear and submission, but it has no power over us, unless we, forgetting our freedom, yield to its temptation and give it power.

We are the Lord's freedmen. "We have our liberty in Christ Jesus." In Romans seven Paul describes the terrible struggles of the soul who still seeks to fulfill the law but finds itself utterly helpless— sold under sin, a captive and a slave, without the liberty to do what the whole heart desires. But when the Spirit takes the place of the law, the complaint "What a wretched man I am" is changed into the song of victory "I thank God, through Christ Jesus the law of the Spirit of life has set me free."

What numberless complaints of insufficient strength to do God's will, of unsuccessful effort and disappointed hopes and continual failure re-echo in a thousand different forms the complaint of the captive, "What a wretched man I am!" Thank God! There *is* deliverance. "With freedom Christ has set us free! Stand fast therefore, and be not entangled again in a yoke of bondage." Satan is always trying to lay on us again either the yoke of sin or the law and to create again the spirit of bondage, as if sin or the law with their demands somehow had power over us. Do not let him ensnare you with these tricks. Stand fast in the liberty with which Christ has made you free. Listen to the message: "You have been set free from sin and have become slaves to righteousness. . . . Now offer [yourself] in slavery to righteousness leading to holiness" (Romans 6:18–19). "Now that you have been set free from sin and have become slaves to God, the benefit you reap leads to holiness" (v. 22). To be holy, you must be free, perfectly free—free for Jesus to rule and lead you; free for the Holy Spirit to work through you, to breathe in you, to work His secret, gentle, but mighty work so that you may mature into all the liberty Jesus has won for you. God cannot sanctify a temple unless it is free from every other master and every other use. It must be for God and His service alone. And so the inner temple of our heart cannot be truly and fully sanctified unless we are free from every other master and power, from every yoke of bondage, fear or doubt, free to let His Spirit lead us into the perfect liberty whose fruit is true holiness.

Being made free from sin, having become servants of righteousness, you have your fruit of holiness and the end is life everlasting. Freedom, righteousness, holiness—these are steps on the way to the coming glory. The more deeply we enter by faith into our liberty that we have in Christ, the more joyfully and confidently we present our members to God as instruments of righteousness. God is the Father whose will we delight to do, whose service is perfect liberty. The Redeemer is the Master, to whom love binds us in willing obedience. The liberty is not lawlessness: "[He] rescue[d] us from the hand of our enemies . . . to enable us to serve him . . . in holiness and righteousness before him all our days" (Luke 1:74–75).

Liberty is the condition of righteousness, and again of holiness. Doing God's will leads to fellowship, wholehearted agreement with God himself, out of which comes the reflection of the divine presence, which is holiness. Being made free from sin, being made the slaves of righteousness and of God, we have our fruit unto holiness, and the end everlasting life.

Most glorious God, I pray you will open my eyes to this wonderful liberty with which Christ has made me free. May I enter fully into your Word that sin shall not have dominion over me because I am not under the law but under grace. May I know the liberty that I have in Christ Jesus and stand fast in it.

Father, your service is perfect liberty: reveal this too to me. You are infinitely free, and your will knows no limits except those its own perfection has required. You invite us into your will that we may be free even as you are. O my God, show me the beauty of your will that can free me from self and sin. Let the service of righteousness be my joy and strength, having its fruit unto sanctification, leading me into your holiness.

Blessed Lord Jesus! my Deliverer and my liberty, I belong to you. I give myself to your will, to know no will but yours. Master! you and you alone would I serve. I have my liberty in you; be my keeper. I cannot stand one moment without you. In you I can stand fast; in you I put my trust. Amen.

Personal Application

1. Liberty is the power to carry out unhindered the impulses of our nature. In Christ the child of God is free from every power that could hinder his acting out the law of his new nature.

2. This liberty is of faith (Galatians 5:5–6). By faith in Christ I enter into this liberty and stand.

3. This liberty is of the Holy Spirit. "Where the Spirit of the Lord is, there is freedom" (2 Corinthians 3:17). "But if you are led by the Spirit, you are not under law" (Galatians 5:18). A heart filled with the Spirit is made free indeed. But we are not made free that we may do our own will. Rather, we are made free to follow the leading of the Holy Spirit. "Where the Spirit is, there is freedom."

4. This liberty is in love. "You . . . were called to be free. But do not use your freedom to indulge the sinful nature; rather, serve one another in love" (Galatians 5:13). The freedom with which the Son makes free is a freedom to become like Him, to love and to serve. "Though I am free and belong to no man, I make myself a slave to everyone, to win as many as possible" (1 Corinthians 9:19). This is the liberty of love.

5. "You have been set free from sin and have become slaves to righteousness" (Romans 6:18). "Let my people go, so that they may worship me" (Exodus 8:1). It is only the man who lives righteously that can become holy.

6. This liberty is a thing of joy and singing.

7. This liberty is the groundwork of holiness. The Redeemer who makes us free is God the Holy One. As the Holy Spirit, He leads us into the full possession of it. To be so free from everything that God can take complete possession is to be holy.

Chapter 21

Holiness and Happiness

For the kingdom of God is . . . joy in the Holy Spirit.

Romans 14:17

The disciples were filled with joy and with the Holy Spirit.

Acts 13:52

Then Nehemiah . . . said . . . "This day is sacred to the Lord your God. Do not mourn or weep . . . for the joy of the Lord is your strength." The Levites calmed all the people, saying, "Be still, for this is a sacred day. Do not grieve." Then all the people went away . . . to celebrate with great joy, because they now understood the words.

Nehemiah 8:9–12

The deep significance of joy in the Christian life is rarely understood. Too often it is regarded as something secondary, whereas its presence is essential as the proof that God does indeed satisfy us and that His service is our delight. In our homelife we do not feel satisfied if only the bare standards of conduct are observed and each only does his duty to the other; true love makes us happy to serve one another over and above what is expected. As love expresses itself in warm affection, gladness is the sunshine that fills the home with its brightness. Even in suffering or poverty, the members of a loving family are a joy to one another. Without this gladness, there is a lack of true obedience on the part of the children. It is not the mere fulfillment of a command or performance of a service that a parent looks for, but the willing, joyful eagerness with which it is done that makes it pleasing.

It is the same in the relationship of God's children with their Father. Even in our effort to live a life of consecration and obedience, we are continually in danger of coming under the law again. The consequence is always failure. The law only works wrath; it gives neither life nor strength. Only as long as we are standing in the joy of our deliverance from sin and the joy of His presence will we have the power to serve and obey. It is only when we are made free from every master, from sin and self and the law, and only when we are rejoicing in this liberty, will we have the power to render service that is satisfying to God and to one another. "I will see you again," Jesus said, "and you will rejoice, and no one will take away your joy" (John 16:22). Joy is the evidence and the condition of the abiding personal presence of Jesus Christ.

If holiness is the beauty and the glory of the life of faith, then it is obvious that here especially the element of joy should not be missing. We have already seen the first mention of God as the Holy One in the song of praise on the shores of the Red Sea; how Hannah and Mary in their moments of inspiration praised God as the Holy One; how the name of the Thrice Holy in heaven comes to us in the song of the seraphs; and how before the throne both the living creatures and the conquering multitude who sing the song of the Lamb, adore God as the Holy One. We are to "worship the Lord in the beauty of holiness" (1 Chronicles 16:29), and to "sing to the Lord [and] praise his holy name" (Psalm 30:4). It is only in the spirit of worship and praise and joy that we can fully know God as holy. Much more, only under the inspiration of adoring love and joy can we be made holy. As we cease from all fear and anxiety, from all strain and effort, and rest with joy in what Jesus is in His finished work as our sanctification, as we rejoice in Him, we shall be made partakers of His holiness. The day of grace is the day of rest, the day God has blessed, a day of blessing and gladness. Holiness and blessedness are inseparable.

Is this contrary to the teaching of Scripture and the experience of the saints? Are suffering and sorrow also among God's chosen means of sanctification? Are the promises made to the broken-hearted, the poor in spirit, and those who mourn? Are not self-denial and forsaking all we have, our crucifixion with Christ and our dying daily, the true path to holiness? Do these requirements bring more sorrow and pain than joy and gladness?

The answer is found in a right understanding of the life of faith. Faith lifts above and gives possession of what is the very opposite of what we feel or experience. In the Christian life there is always a paradox: things that appear to be irreconcilable opposites are found side by side at the same moment. Paul expresses it in the words "dying, and yet we live on ... sorrowful, yet always rejoicing; poor, yet making many rich; having nothing, and yet possessing everything" (2 Corinthians 6:9–10). And elsewhere, "When I am weak, then I am strong" (2 Corinthians 12:10). The apparent contradiction has its reconciliation not only in the union of the two lives—the human and the divine—in the person of each believer, but especially in our being simultaneously partakers of the death and the resurrection of Christ. Christ's death was certainly one of pain and suffering, a real and terrible death, a rending asunder of the bonds that united soul and body, spirit and flesh. The power of that death works in us. We must let it work mightily if we are to live holy lives, for in that death He sanctified himself that we ourselves might be sanctified in truth. Like His, our holiness is found in death to our own will and our own life.

But we must understand: we do not approach death from the same side as Christ did, as an enemy to be conquered, as a suffering to be borne, before the new life can be entered into. The believer who knows who Christ is as the Risen One approaches death, the crucifixion of self and the flesh and the world, from the resurrection side, the place of victory, in the power of the living Christ. When we were baptized into Christ, we were baptized into His death and resurrection as our own, and Christ himself, the risen, living Lord, leads us triumphantly into the experience of the power of His death. To the believer who truly lives by faith and does not try by his own efforts to crucify and mortify the flesh, but knows the living Lord, the deep resurrection joy never forsakes Him. Instead, that joy is his strength for what may appear to others to be only painful sacrifice and bearing of a cross. He says with Paul, "I glory in the cross through which I have been crucified." He never, as so many do, asks Paul's question, "Who will rescue me from this body of death?" (Romans 7:24) without giving the joyful and triumphant answer as a present experience: "Thanks be to God—through Jesus Christ our Lord" (Romans 7:25); "But thanks be to God! He gives us the victory through our Lord Jesus Christ" (1 Corinthians 15:57). It is only the joy of a present Savior, the experience of a perfect salvation, and the joy of a resurrection life that gives the power to enter deeply and fully into the death that Christ died and to yield our will and our life to be wholly sanctified to God. In the joy of that life from which the power of death is never absent, it is possible to say with the Apostle each moment, "dying, and yet we live on . . . sorrowful, yet always rejoicing" (2 Corinthians 6:9–10).

Let us seek to learn the two lessons: Holiness is essential to true happiness; happiness is essential to true holiness.

Holiness is essential to true happiness. If you would have joy, the fullness of joy, an abiding joy that nothing can take away, be holy as God is holy. Holiness is blessedness. Nothing but sin can darken or interrupt our joy. Whatever our trial or temptation is, the joy of Jesus of which Peter says, "You believe in him and are filled with an inexpressible and glorious joy" (1 Peter 1:8), can more than compensate. If we lose our joy, it must be because of sin. It may be an actual transgression or an unconscious following of self or the world. It may be the stain on our conscience of something doubtful. Or perhaps it is unbelief that wants to live by sight and thinks more of itself and its joy than of the Lord alone. Whatever it is, remember that nothing can take away our joy except sin. If we would live lives of joy, assuring God and man and ourselves that our Lord is more than anything or everything to us, then be holy! Glory in Him who is our holiness; in His presence is fullness of joy. Live in the kingdom that is joy in the Holy Spirit. The Spirit of holiness is the Spirit of joy because He is the Spirit of God. The saints, God's holy ones, are those who will shout for joy.

Happiness is essential to true holiness. If you want to be a holy Christian, you must be a happy Christian. Jesus was anointed with the oil of joy that He might give us "the oil of joy" (Hebrews 1:9). In all our efforts after holiness, the wheels will move heavily if there is no oil of joy; this alone removes all strain and friction, and makes the onward progress easy and delightful. Study to understand the divine value of joy. It is the evidence of your being in the Father's presence and dwelling in His love. Joy is the proof of your being consciously free from the law and the strain of the spirit of bondage. Joy is the token of your freedom from care and responsibility, because you are rejoicing in Christ Jesus as your sanctification, your keeper and your strength. The secret of spiritual health and strength is joy, filling all your service with the happy, childlike assurance that the Father asks nothing for which He does not give strength, and that He accepts all that is done—however weakly—in this spirit.

True happiness is always self-forgetful; it loses itself in the object of its joy. As the joy of the Holy Spirit fills us and we rejoice in God the Holy One through our Lord Jesus Christ, as we lose ourselves in the adoration and worship of the Thrice Holy, we become holy. Even here in the wilderness this is "called the Way of Holiness. . . . The ransomed of the Lord will return . . . with singing; everlasting joy will crown their heads. Gladness and joy will overtake them" (Isaiah 35:8, 10).

I wonder if God's children understand that holiness is another name God gives to happiness? To know that God makes us holy, that our holiness is in Christ, and that Christ's Holy Spirit is within us, is blessedness beyond description. Nothing is so attractive as joy. Do we understand that this is the joy of the Lord—to be holy? Or is the idea of strain, sacrifice, and sighing, of difficulty and distance so prevalent that the thought of being holy rarely makes the heart glad? If this has been true, let it no longer be so. "You will . . . glory in the Holy One of Israel" (Isaiah 41:16). Claim this promise. Believe that our loving Father, our beloved Lord Jesus, and the Holy Spirit, who in dovelike gentleness rests within us, have undertaken the work and are doing it. Let that assurance fill us with gladness. What we see in ourselves of holiness is not where we must look for joy—let us rejoice in the holiness of God in Christ as ours, let us rejoice in the Holy One of Israel. So shall our joy be unspeakable and unceasing; so shall we give Him the glory.

Blessed God, I ask you to reveal to me and to all your children the secret of rejoicing in you, the Holy One of Israel. You see how much service is still in the spirit of bondage, and how many do not yet believe that the highway of holiness is one on which they may walk with singing and where they shall obtain joy and gladness. O Father, teach your children to rejoice in you.

Teach us that in deep poverty of spirit, in humility and contrition and utter emptiness, in the consciousness that there is no holiness in us, we can sing all day of your holiness as ours, of your glory that you place upon us. O Father, open wide to your children the blessed mystery of the kingdom, the faith that sees all in Christ and nothing in itself.

In your Word you have said, "The meek also shall increase their joy in the Lord, and the poor among men shall rejoice in the Holy One of Israel." Help us, by your Holy Spirit, in meekness and poverty of spirit, to so live in Christ that His holiness may be our true joy, and that in yourself, the Holy One of Israel, we may rejoice always. Amen.

Personal Application

1. The great hindrance to joy in God is expecting to find something in ourselves over which to rejoice. At the beginning of this pursuit of holiness we always expect to see a great change in us. As we are led deeper and see what faith and the faith-life are, we understand that although we do not see the change we expected, still we may rejoice with joy unspeakable in what Jesus is and has done. This is the secret of holiness.

2. Joy must be cultivated. To rejoice is a command more frequently given than we may realize. It is part of the obedience of faith, to rejoice when we do not feel like doing so. Faith rejoices and sings because God is holy.

3. "Filled with joy and the Holy Spirit" (Acts 13:52); "The kingdom of God is . . . joy in the Holy Spirit" (Romans 14:17). The Holy Spirit, the Blessed Spirit of Jesus, is within you, a fountain of living water, of joy and gladness. Seek to know Him who dwells in you, to work out all that Jesus has for you. He will be in you the Spirit of faith and joy.

4. Love and joy always keep company. Love, denying and forgetting itself for the brethren and the lost, living in them, finds the joy of God. "The kingdom of God is . . . joy in the Holy Spirit."

Chapter 22

In Christ Our Sanctification

It is because of [God] that you are in Christ Jesus, who has
become for us wisdom from God—that is, our righteousness,
holiness, and redemption. Therefore, as it is written:
"Let him who boasts boast in the Lord."

1 Corinthians 1:30–31

These words lead us to the very center of God's revelation of the way of holiness. We know the steps on the road that lead here. He is holy; holiness is His. He makes holy by coming near. His presence is holiness. In Christ's life, the holiness that before had only been revealed in symbol and as a promise of good things to come, took possession of a human will and was made one with human nature. In His death every obstacle was removed that could prevent the transmission of that holy nature to us: Christ truly became our sanctification. In the Holy Spirit the actual communication of that holiness took place. We want to understand what the work is that the Holy Spirit does and how He communicates this holy nature to us. We want to know what our relationship is to Christ as our sanctification and what position we must take toward Him so that His power can work in us.

We need to understand what this life in Christ is and how on our part it may be accepted and maintained. Of this we may be sure, it is not something beyond our reach. There need not be any exhausting effort or hopeless sighing, "Who will ascend into heaven? (that is, to bring Christ down)" (Romans 10:6). This life is meant for the sinful and the weary, for the unworthy and the impotent. It is a life that is the gift of the Father's love and a life that He will reveal in each one who comes in childlike trust to Him. It is a life that is meant for our everyday life. In every varying circumstance and situation this life will make and keep us holy.

Before our Lord left the world, He said, "And surely I am with you always, to the very end of the age" (Matthew 28:20). And it is written of Him: "He who descended is the very one who ascended higher than all the heavens, in order to fill the whole universe" (Ephesians 4:10). "The church . . . is his body, the fullness of him who fills everything in every way" (Ephesians 1:22–23). In the Holy Spirit the Lord Jesus is with His people here on earth. Though unseen and not in the flesh, His personal presence is as real on earth as when He walked with His disciples. In regeneration the believer is taken out of his old place "in the flesh." He is no longer in the flesh, but in the spirit (Romans 8:9). He is actually in Christ. The living Christ is around him by His holy presence. Wherever and whatever he is, however ignorant of his position or however unfaithful to it, he is in Christ. By an act of divine and omnipotent grace, he has been planted into Christ, encircled on every side by the power and the love of Him who fills all things, whose fullness dwells in His body here below, the church.

How can one who longs to know Christ fully as his sanctification live out what God has provided "in Christ"? The first thing to remember is that it is of faith and not feeling. The promise of the indwelling and quickening of the Holy One is to the humble and the contrite. Just when I feel most deeply that I am not holy and can do nothing to make myself holy, when I feel I have failed, that is the time to turn from self and quietly say, "I am in Christ. He is all around me. Like the air that surrounds me, like the light that shines on me, here is my Lord Jesus with me in His hidden but divine and most real presence. My faith must in quiet rest and trust bow before the Father, of whom and by whose mighty grace I am in Christ." He will reveal this to me with ever-growing clarity and power. He does it as I believe, and in believing I open my whole soul to receive what is implied in it: the sense of my own sinfulness and *un*holiness must become the strength of my trust and dependence. In such faith I abide in Christ.

But because it is of faith, it is of the Holy Spirit. Of God we are in Christ. It is not as if God placed and planted us in Christ and then left it to us to maintain the union. God is the Eternal One, the God of everlasting life, who works every moment in a power that does not for one moment cease. What God gives, He continues to give unceasingly. It is He, by the Holy Spirit, who makes this life in Christ a blessed reality. "We have . . . received . . . the Spirit who is from God, that we may understand what God has freely given us" (1 Corinthians 2:12). Faith is not only dependent on God for the gift it is to accept but also for the power to accept it. Faith not only needs the Son as its filling and its food, it needs the Spirit as its power to receive and hold fast. And so the blessed possession of all that it means to be in Christ, our sanctification, comes as we learn to bow before God in believing prayer for the mighty workings of the Spirit, and in deep childlike trust know that He will reveal and glorify Christ in us.

How will the Spirit reveal Christ? It will be as the living One, the personal friend and master. Christ is not only our example and our ideal. His life is not only an atmosphere and an inspiration such as we might say about a man who influences us by his writing. Christ is not only a treasury and a fullness of grace and power into which the Spirit is to lead us, but Christ is the living Savior, with a heart that beats with a love that is most tenderly human and yet divine. In this love He comes very near to us and receives us. In the power of a personal love, He longs to exercise His influence and unite us to himself. In this love we have the guarantee that His holiness will be our holiness. As the Spirit reveals to us where we are dwelling— in Christ and His love—and that this Christ is a living Lord and Savior, there will awaken within us the enthusiasm of a personal attachment and the devotion of a loving allegiance that will make us wholly His. Seeing this, it becomes possible for us to believe that we can be holy. We feel a certainty that in the path of holiness we can go from strength to strength.

Such insight into our relationship to Christ as being in Him, and such personal attachment to Him who has received us into His love and keeps us abiding there, becomes the source of a new obedience. The will of God comes to us in the light of Christ's life and His love—each command first fulfilled by Him, and then passed on to us as the sure and blessed help to more perfect fellowship with the Father and His holiness. In the power of the Holy Spirit, Christ becomes Lord and King in the soul, guiding our will into the perfect will of God, proving himself to be our sanctification as He crowns our obedience with an ever-widening flow of the presence and holiness of God.

Are you discouraged as you think of living a holy life? Do not be. God could not have devised anything more wonderful or beautiful than He has for His sinful, impotent creatures. Imagine, Christ—God's own Son—made to be sanctification in you. The mighty, loving, holy Christ was sanctified through suffering that He might have sympathy with you. He was given to make you holy. Could you possibly desire more? Whether you understand it or not, however faintly you realize it, the fact is divinely true and real. You are in Christ by an act of God's own mighty power. And God himself longs to establish and confirm you there, in Christ, to the end. The greatest wonder of all is that you have the Holy Spirit within you to teach you to know and believe and receive all that there is in Christ for you. If you will only confess that there is in you no wisdom or power for holiness and allow Christ, "the wisdom of God and the power of God," to lead you by the Holy Spirit and prove how completely, faithfully, and mightily He can be your sanctification, He will do it.

Come and yield more fully to God's way of holiness. Let Christ be your sanctification. Not a distant Christ to whom you look but a Christ who is near, all around you, in you. Not a Christ after the flesh, a Christ of the past, but a present Christ in the power of the Holy Spirit. Not a Christ whom you can know by your wisdom, but the Christ of God who is the Spirit within you. Not a limited Christ—one your finite mind might conceive of—but a Christ according to the greatness of the heart and love of God. Come and accept this Christ and rejoice in Him! Be content to leave all your weakness, foolishness, and faithlessness to Him in the quiet confidence that He will do for you more than you could ever ask or think. And so from now on let it be as it is written: He that glories, let him glory in the Lord.

Most blessed Father, I bow in speechless adoration before the holy mystery of your divine love. Forgive me that I have known and believed in your love so much less than it deserves to be known and believed. Accept my praise for what I have seen and tasted of its divine blessedness. Accept, Lord God, the praise of a glad and loving heart that knows it can never praise you enough.

Hear my prayer, O Father, that in the power of your Holy Spirit who dwells in me, I may each day accept and live out fully what you have given me in Christ. May the unsearchable riches there are in Him be the daily supply for my every need. May His holiness, His delight in your will, indeed become mine. Teach me, above all, how this can be, because I am, through the work of your almighty quickening power, kept there by you alone.

In this faith I yield myself to you, Lord Jesus, my King and Master, to do your will. In everything I do, great or small, I would act as one sanctified in Jesus, united to God's will in Him. You alone can teach me to do this, can give me strength to perform it. You are my sanctification. I trust you. Amen.

Personal Application

1. Christ, as He lived and died on earth, is our sanctification. His life, the Spirit of His life, is what constitutes our holiness. To be in perfect harmony with Christ, to have His mind, is to be holy.
2. Christ's holiness had two sides. God sanctified Him by His Spirit; Christ sanctified himself by following the leading of the Spirit, by giving up His will to God in everything. So God has made us holy in Christ; and so we follow after and perfect holiness by yielding ourselves to God's Spirit, by giving up our will and living in the will of God.
3. We would do well to take in every aspect of what God has revealed of holiness in His Word. But let us never weary ourselves by seeking to grasp it all completely. Let us return to the simplicity that is in Jesus. To bow at His feet, to believe that He knows all we need and has it all—and loves to give it to us. Holiness is resting in Jesus, the rest of God.
4. This holy life in Christ is for today. Today He will be your holiness. Believe in Him for it, trust Him, and praise Him. And remember: *You are in Him.*

Holiness and the Body

God's temple is sacred, and you are that temple. . . . The body is . . . for the Lord; and the Lord for the body. . . . Do you not know that your body is a temple of the Holy Spirit, who is in you? . . . Therefore honor God with your body.

1 Corinthians 3:17; 6:13, 19–20

An unmarried woman or virgin is concerned about the Lord's affairs: Her aim is to be devoted to the Lord in both body and spirit.

1 Corinthians 7:34

Offer your bodies as living sacrifices, holy and pleasing to God.

Romans 12:1

Coming into the world, our blessed Lord said, "A body you pre-pared for me; here I am, I have come to do your will, O God." Leaving this world again, it was in His own body that He bore our sins upon the tree. So it was in the body, no less than in soul and spirit, that He did the will of God. And therefore it is said, "And by that will, we have been made holy through the sacrifice of the body of Jesus Christ once for all" (Hebrews 10:10).

When praying for the Thessalonians and their sanctification, Paul says, "May God himself, the God of peace, sanctify you through and through. May your whole spirit, soul and body be kept blameless at the coming of our Lord Jesus Christ" (1 Thessalonians 5:23). Of himself he had spoken as "always carry around in our body the death of Jesus, so that the life of Jesus may also be revealed in our body. For we who are alive are always being given over to death for Jesus' sake, so that his life may be revealed in our mortal body" (2 Corinthians 4:10–11). His earnest expectation and hope was "Christ will be exalted in my body, whether by life or by death" (Philippians 1:20). The relationship between the body and the spirit is so intimate, the power of sin in the spirit so influential on the body, and the body so distinctly the object both of Christ's redemption and the Holy Spirit's renewal, that our study of holiness will be seriously deficient if we do not take into consideration the teaching of Scripture on holiness in the body.

A good comparison is that the body is around the soul and spirit like the walls of a city. Through them the enemy may enter. In time of war, the defense of the walls is of prime importance. Because the believer does not know the importance of keeping the walls defended by keeping the body sanctified, he often fails to keep the soul and spirit preserved blameless. Or perhaps he does not understand that the guarding and sanctifying of the body in all its parts must be a distinct work of faith. It must be accomplished directly through the mighty power of Jesus and the indwelling of the Spirit, just as is the renewing of the inner life. Is it because he does not know this fact that progress is slow? The rule of the city we entrust to Jesus, but the defense of the walls is in our own hands. The King does not keep us as we expected and we cannot discover the secret of failure. It is the God of peace himself who sanctifies wholly, who must preserve spirit and soul and body complete and without blame. The tabernacle, with its wood and its stone, was as holy as all that was included within its walls. And God's holy ones need the body to maintain holiness.

To fully understand this, let us remember it was through the body that sin entered. "The woman saw that the fruit of the tree was good for food"; this was a temptation to the flesh. Through this the soul was reached: "pleasing to the eye." Through the soul it then passed into the spirit: "and also desirable for gaining wisdom" (Genesis 3:6). In John's description of what is in the world (1 John 2:16), we find the same threefold division: "the cravings of sinful man, the lust of his eyes and the boasting of what he has and does." The three temptations of Jesus by Satan correspond exactly: he first sought to reach Him through the body, suggesting he satisfy His hunger by making bread; the second (see Luke 4) appealed to the soul, in the vision of the kingdoms of this world and their glory; the third to the spirit, in the call to assert and prove His divine sonship by casting himself down. Even to the Son of God the first temptation came, just as to Adam and to all in the world: the desire to gratify the natural and lawful appetite of hunger. It was on a question of eating what appeared good for food that man's first sin was committed, and that same question of eating to satisfy hunger was the battleground on which the Redeemer's first encounter with Satan took place. Many Christians are unknowingly tripped up by Satan on the question of eating and drinking what is lawful and good. To have every appetite of the body under the rule and regulation of the Holy Spirit appears to some unnecessary, to others too difficult. And yet it must be so if the body is to be holy, as God's temple, and we are to glorify Him in our body and our spirit. The first attack of sin is made through the body; in the body the complete victory will be gained.

Physiology confirms what Scripture teaches about the intimacy that exists between the body and the spirit. Things that appear at first to be merely physical transgressions leave a mark and have a degrading influence on the soul, and through it drag down the spirit. On the other hand, spiritual sins—sins of thought and imagination and disposition—pass through the soul into the body, fix themselves in the nervous system, and express themselves even in the countenance and the habits or tendencies of the body. If we are to perfect holiness, we must cleanse ourselves from all defilement of the spirit *and* the body. "If by the Spirit you put to death the misdeeds of the body, you will live" (Romans 8:13). If we are indeed to be cleansed from sin and made holy unto God, the body as the outer defense must be well protected from the power of Satan and of sin.

God has made very special provision for this. The Scriptures speak explicitly of the Holy Spirit's communicating holiness in connection with the body. At first glance, it looks as if the expression "your bodies" was simply used as an equivalent to "your persons," or "your selves." But as insight deepens into the power of sin in the body, our perception of the body as a temple of the Holy Spirit is sharpened. We notice that it is particularly sins of the body that Paul says defile God's temple, and how it is through the power of the Holy Spirit in the body that he would have us glorify God. "Do you not know that your body is a temple of the Holy Spirit? . . . Therefore honor God with your body" (1 Corinthians 6:19–20). The Holy Spirit must not only exercise a restraining and regulating influence on the appetites of the body so that they are in moderation—this is only the negative side—but there must be a positive spiritual element, making the exercise of natural functions a service of holy joy and liberty to the glory of God. No longer need they be a threatening hindrance to the life of obedience and fellowship, but instead a means of grace, a help to the spiritual life. Only in a body that is full of God's Spirit will this be possible.

How can this change be accomplished? In the true Christian life, self-denial is the path to enjoyment. As long as there is anything that we think we have liberty to use or enjoy—even in moderation—we have not yet seen or confessed our own need of total renewal by the Holy Spirit. It is not enough to say, "Everything God created is good . . . if it is received with thanksgiving" (1 Timothy 4:4); we must remember the addition, "because it is consecrated by the word of God and prayer" (1 Timothy 4:5). This sanctifying of everything and its use is as real and solemn as the sanctifying of ourselves. If need be, we must sacrifice the gift and the liberty to use it, until God gives us the freedom to use it to His glory alone. Even speaking of the most sacred of divine institutions—marriage—Paul (who denounced those who forbid to marry) says distinctly that there may be cases in which a voluntary celibacy may be the surest and most acceptable way of being "holy both in body and spirit." When to be holy as God is holy becomes the overwhelming desire and aim of life, everything will either be cherished or surrendered according to whether it promotes that supreme purpose. The actual and active presence of the Holy Spirit in the life of the body will be the fire that burns continually on the altar.

With the body, as it is with the spirit, it is God who works; God in Christ is our keeper and our sanctifier. The guarding of the walls of the city must be entrusted to Him who rules within. "[I] am convinced that he is able to guard what I have entrusted to him" (2 Timothy 1:12), to keep that which I have committed to Him. This must become as true of the body and its functions that have caused doubt or stumbling as it has been true of the soul we entrusted to Him for salvation. A fixed deposit in a bank is money given away for safekeeping. Likewise, the body or any part of it that needs to be made holy must be committed to Jesus as a deposit. Faith must trust His acceptance and safekeeping; prayer and praise must daily renew the assurance, confirm the deposit, and maintain the fellowship with Jesus. Abiding in Him and His holiness in a life of trust and joy, we shall receive the power to prove, even in the body, how fully and wholly we are in Him who is made unto us sanctification. We shall prove how real and true the holiness of God is in His people.

Blessed Lord, you who are my sanctification, I come to you with a special request. In your own body you bore our sins on the tree, and it is written of you, "We have been made holy through the sacrifice of the body of Jesus Christ once for all." Reveal to me how my body may experience the power of your wonderful redemption. I desire in soul and body to be holy unto the Lord.

I have not fully understood that my body is the temple of the Holy Spirit and that nothing in it can be a matter of indifference. Even when I realized this, I still sought to guard these walls of the city from the Enemy's attacks by myself. I forgot that this part of my being could be kept and sanctified only by faith, by your taking charge and keeping what I have entrusted to you.

I come now to surrender this body with all its needs into your hands. In weariness and in pain, in joy and in laughter, in hunger and in want, in health and in plenty, let my body be in your keeping every moment. Whether I live or die, magnify yourself in my body. Amen.

Personal Application

1. In the tabernacle and the temple, the material part was to be in harmony with and the embodiment of the holiness that dwelt within. It was, therefore, all made according to the pattern shown on the mount. In the two last chapters of Exodus, we have eighteen times "as the Lord commanded." Everything, even in the exterior, was the embodiment of the will of God. Even so our body, as God's temple, must in everything be regulated by God's Word, quickened and sanctified by the Holy Spirit.

2. As part of this holiness in the body, Scripture mentions dress. Speaking of the "outward adornment, such as braided hair and the wearing of gold jewelry and fine clothes," as inconsistent with

"the unfading beauty of a gentle and quiet spirit," Peter says, "For this is the way the holy women of the past who put their hope in God used to make themselves beautiful" (1 Peter 3:3–5). Holiness was seen even in their dress; their body was the temple of the Holy Spirit.

3. "If by the Spirit you put to death the misdeeds of the body, you will live" (Romans 8:13). His quickening energy must reign throughout. We are so accustomed to connecting the spiritual with the ideal and the invisible that it will take time and thought and faith to realize how the physical and the sensible influence our spiritual life and must be under the mastery and inspiration of God's Spirit. Even Paul says, "I beat my body and make it my slave so . . . I myself will not be disqualified for the prize" (1 Corinthians 9:27).

4. If God actually breathed His Spirit into the body of Adam, formed out of the ground, let it not be thought strange that the Holy Spirit should now animate our bodies with His sanctifying energy.

5. "Corporeality is the end of the ways of God." This saying of an old divine reminds us of a much-neglected truth. The great work of God's Spirit is to ally himself with matter and form it into a spiritual body for His dwelling. The Holy Spirit will do this in our bodies if He gains complete possession. But He will not dwell in an unwilling body. That is up to us.

6. It is on this truth of the Holy Spirit's power in the body that faith healing rests. Through all ages, in times of special spiritual awakening, God has allowed some to see how Christ would make, even here, the body a partaker of the life and power of the Spirit. To those who do see it, the link between holiness and healing is a very close and blessed one as the Lord Jesus takes possession of the body for himself.

Chapter 24

Holiness and Cleansing

Since we have these promises, dear friends, let us purify ourselves
from everything that contaminates body and spirit, perfecting
holiness out of reverence for God.

2 Corinthians 7:1

More than one passage in the New Testament teaches that holiness is more than cleansing and must be preceded by it. "Christ loved the church and gave himself up for her to make her holy, cleansing her by the washing with water through the word" (Ephesians 5:25–26). "If a man cleanses himself . . . he will be . . . made holy" (2 Timothy 2:21). Cleansing is the negative side, washing away defilement; being separate and not touching the unclean thing is the avoidance of impurity; sanctification is the positive union and fellowship with God and the participation of the graces of the divine life and holiness (2 Corinthians 6:17–18). Of the altar we read that God said to Moses: "Purify the altar by making atonement for it, and anoint it to consecrate it" (Exodus 29:36). Cleansing, then, prepares the way, and should always lead on to holiness.

Paul speaks of a twofold defilement of flesh and spirit from which we must cleanse ourselves. The connection between the two is so close that in the instance of every sin both flesh and spirit are partakers. The lowest and most carnal form of sin will enter the spirit, defiling it and degrading it. So also will all defilement of the spirit in time show its influence in the flesh. We may still speak of the two types of sin, depending on whether its origin is directly related to the flesh or to the spirit.

"Let us purify ourselves from everything that contaminates body and spirit" (2 Corinthians 7:1). The functions of our body may be categorized under three headings: the nourishment, the propagation, and the protection of our life. Through the first, the world daily appeals to our appetite for food and drink. Just as the fruit that appeared good for food was the temptation that overcame Eve, so the pleasures of eating and drinking are among the earliest forms of defilement of the flesh. Closely connected with this are the functions of the second category, which in Scripture are especially connected with the word *flesh*. We remember how in the Garden, the partaking of the forbidden fruit was followed closely by the awakening of lust and shame in the couple. In Corinthians, Paul closely connects the two (1 Corinthians 6:13, 15), as he also links drunkenness and impurity (1 Corinthians 6:9–10). Then follows the third category, in which the vitality of the body displays itself: the instinct of self-preservation setting itself against everything that interferes with its pleasure and comfort. What we call "temper," with its fruits of anger and strife, has its roots in the physical constitution and is among the many sins of the flesh. From all these things, the Christian who would be holy must resolutely cleanse himself. He must yield himself to the searching of God's Spirit to be taught what in the flesh is not in harmony with the temperance and self-control required both by the laws of nature and of the Spirit. He must believe what Paul felt the Corinthians so emphatically needed to be taught, that the Holy Spirit dwells in the body, making its members the members of Christ; and in this faith he must put off the works of the flesh; he must cleanse himself from all defilement of the flesh.

Just as the source of all defilement of the flesh is self-gratification, so self-seeking is at the root of all defilement of the spirit. In relation to God, it manifests itself in idolatry, whether it is in the worship of other gods, the love of the world, or doing our will rather than His will. In relation to others, it shows itself in envy, hatred, a lack of love, cold neglect, or harsh judgment. In relation to ourselves, it is seen as pride, selfish ambition, envy, and the disposition that makes self the center around which all must move and by which all must be judged.

For the discovery of such defilement of the spirit, no less than of the sins of the flesh, the believer needs the light of the Holy Spirit so that the uncleanness may be discovered, cleansed, and put away. Even unconscious sin, if we are not willing to have it shown to us, will prevent our progress in the path of holiness.

"Dear friends, let us purify ourselves" (2 Corinthians 7:1). The cleansing is sometimes spoken of as the work of God (Acts 15:9; 1 John 1:9) and sometimes as that of Christ (John 15:3; Ephesians 5:26; Titus 2:14). Here we are commanded to cleanse ourselves. God does His work in us by the Holy Spirit. The Spirit does His work by stirring us up and enabling us to do what we must. The Spirit is the strength of the new life; in that strength we must set ourselves determinedly to cast out whatever is unclean. "Come out from them and be separate, says the Lord. Touch no unclean thing" (2 Corinthians 6:17). It is not only doing what is sinful that the Christian must avoid but even coming near to what is sinful. The involuntary contact with it must be so unbearable as to force the cry, "What a wretched man I am!" (Romans 7:24), and to lead on to the deliverance the Spirit of the life of Christ brings.

How is this cleansing to be done? When Hezekiah called the priests to sanctify the temple that had been defiled, we read, "The priests went into the sanctuary of the Lord to purify it. They brought out to the courtyard of the Lord's temple everything unclean that they found in the temple of the Lord" (2 Chronicles 29:16). Only then could the sin offering of atonement and the burnt offering of consecration, with the thank offerings, be brought and God's service be restored. In this same way, all that is unclean must be searched out and brought to the light so that it can be cast out. However deeply rooted the sin may appear, in constitution or in habit, we must cleanse ourselves of it if we would be holy. "If we walk in the light, as he is in the light . . . the blood of Jesus, his Son, purifies us from all sin" (1 John 1:7). As we bring out every sin from the inner part of the "house" and into the light of God, and walk in that light, the precious blood that justifies will also cleanse. The blood brings it into living contact with the life and the love of God. Let us come into the light with our sins. The blood will prove its mighty power. Let us cleanse ourselves by yielding ourselves to the light to reveal and condemn, and to the blood to cleanse and sanctify.

"Let us purify ourselves . . . perfecting holiness out of reverence for God" (2 Corinthians 7:1). We read in Hebrews 10:14, "[Christ] has made perfect forever those who are being made holy." We have often seen that what God has made holy, man must also make holy by accepting and appropriating the holiness God has given. So it is with the perfection the saints have in Christ. We must perfect holiness: holiness must be carried out into the whole of life, even to its end. As God's holy ones, we must go on to perfection. Do not be afraid of the expression our blessed Lord used when He gave us the command "Be perfect, therefore, as your heavenly Father is perfect" (Matthew 5:48). A young person who strives after perfection in the knowledge of a profession he hopes to attain when he has finished school, will be told by his teachers that the way to perfection is to seek to do his best in the lessons of *each day*. To be perfect in each small detail of a work is the path to the perfection that will crown the whole project or endeavor. The Master calls us to a perfection that is like that of the Father. He has already perfected us in himself. He holds out the prospect of an ever-growing perfection. His Word tells us to perfect holiness day by day. Let us seek in each duty to be wholehearted and complete. As teachable scholars, let us in every act of worship or obedience, and in every temptation or trial, do the very best God's Spirit enables us to do. "Perseverance must finish its work so that you may be mature and complete, not lacking anything" (James 1:4). "The God of peace ... equip you with everything good for doing his will" (Hebrews 13:20–21).

"Since we have these promises, dear friends, let us purify ourselves from everything that contaminates body and spirit, perfecting holiness out of reverence for God" (2 Corinthians 7:1). Faith gives the courage and the power to cleanse from all defilement, perfecting holiness in the fear of God. As the Holy Spirit makes the promises of love and indwelling (2 Corinthians 6:16–18) ours, we will share the victory that overcomes the world, even our faith. From the beginning, in the Garden of Eden, down through all of Scripture, we have seen the wondrous revelation of these promises of God in ever-growing splendor. God *will* make us holy and God *will* dwell with the humble. God has planted us in Christ that He may be our sanctification. God has given us the Holy Spirit and watches over us in His love to work out through us His purposes and to perfect our holiness. Such are the promises that have been set plainly before us.

Let us arise and claim by faith the promises, being fully persuaded that what He has promised He is able also to perform. In Christ your strength, yield yourself in faith to perfect the holiness to which you are called. As your Father in heaven is perfect, give yourself to Him as a child to be perfect in your daily lessons and in your daily walk. Believe that your surrender is accepted, that the charge committed to Him is undertaken. And give glory to Him who is able to do abundantly above what you can ask or think.

Holy Lord Jesus, you gave yourself for us so that after cleansing us as your own you might sanctify us and present us to yourself a glorious church, not having spot or wrinkle or any such thing. Blessed be your name for that wonderful love. Blessed be your name for the wonderful cleansing. Through the washing by the Word and the washing in the blood, you have made us clean. And as we walk in the light, you cleanse us every moment.

Armed with these promises and in the power of your Word and blood, you call us to cleanse ourselves from all defilement of flesh and spirit. Blessed Lord, graciously reveal in your holy light all that is defiled, even its most secret working. Let me live as one who is to be presented to you without spot or wrinkle or any such thing—cleansed with a divine cleansing. Under the living power of your Word and blood, applied by the Holy Spirit, may my way be clean, my hands clean, my lips clean, and my heart clean. Cleanse me thoroughly that I may walk with you in holiness here on earth, keeping my garments unspotted and undefiled. For the sake of your great love, I pray, my blessed Lord. Amen.

Personal Application

1. Cleansing has almost always one aim: a cleansed vessel that is fit for use. Spiritual work done for God with the honest desire that He through His Spirit might use us, will give urgency to our desire for cleansing. A vessel that is not cleansed cannot be used. This is the reason there are some workers whom God cannot bless.

2. All it takes to be defiled is one stain. "Let us purify ourselves from everything that contaminates."

3. There is no cleansing without light. Open your heart for the light to shine in and do its work.

4. There is no cleansing like fire. Give any defilement over to the fire of His holiness, the fire that consumes and purifies. Give it

over to the death of Jesus, even to Jesus himself.

5. Rejoice with trembling—work out your salvation with fear and trembling.

6. It is a blessed thing to be cleansed—entering into the promises, the purity, and the love of our Lord. The fear of God need never hinder our faith in Him. And true faith will never hinder the practical work of cleansing.

7. If we walk in the light, the blood cleanses us. The light reveals; we confess and forsake and then accept the cleansing blood. Let there always be a determined purpose to be clean from all defilement, everything that our Father considers sinful or defiling.

Holy and Blameless

You are witnesses, and so is God, of how holy, righteous and blameless we were among you who believed. . . . May the Lord make your love increase and overflow for each other and for everyone else. . . . May he strengthen your hearts so that you will be blameless and holy in the presence of our God and Father when our Lord Jesus comes with all his holy ones.

1 Thessalonians 2:10; 3:12–13

For he chose us in him before the creation of the world to be holy and blameless in his sight.

Ephesians 1:4

Two Greek words, signifying nearly the same thing, are used frequently along with the word *holy*, and following it, to express what the result and effect of holiness will be as manifested in the visible life. The one is translated "unblemished," and is also used of our Lord and His sacrifice: the Lamb without blemish or defect (Hebrews 9:14; 1 Peter 1:19). It is then used of God's children with *holy*—"holy and without blemish or fault." (Luke 1:6; Ephesians 1:4; 5:27; Philippians 2:15; 3:6; Colossians 1:22; 2 Peter 3:14; Jude 24). The other word is translated "blameless" and is also found in conjunction with *holy* (1 Thessalonians 2:10; 3:13; 5:23). To answer the question as to whether "blameless" refers to God's estimate of the saints or man's, Scripture clearly connects it with both. In some passages (Ephesians 1:4; 5:27; Colossians 1:22; 1 Thessalonians 3:13; 2 Peter 3:14) the words "in his sight" and "to himself" and "in the presence of our God and Father" indicate that the first thought is to be spotless and blameless in the presence of a Holy God. In others (Philippians 2:15; 1 Thessalonians 2:10), blamelessness in the sight of men stands to the forefront. In each case the word may be considered to include both aspects: without blemish and without blame must stand the double test of the judgment of God and man.

What lesson does the linking together of these two words in Scripture, and the exposition of "holy" by the addition of "blameless," teach us? It is a lesson of great importance. In the pursuit of holiness, the believer faces a certain danger. The more clearly he realizes what a deep spiritual blessing it is to be found separate from the world and in fellowship with God, to be possessed through a divine indwelling, the more danger he faces of looking too exclusively to the divine side of the blessing in its heavenly and supernatural aspect. He may forget how repentance and obedience, as the paths leading up to holiness, must cover every minute detail of daily life. He may not see that faithfulness to the leading of the Spirit—even to His faintest whisper—in reference to ordinary conduct, is essential if we are to go on to a fuller experience of His power and work as the Spirit of holiness.

He may not have learned that more than obedience to what he knows to be God's will is necessary, as is a very tender and willing teachableness to receive all that the Spirit has to show him of his imperfections and the Father's perfect will concerning him. That teachableness is the only condition on which the holiness of God can be more fully revealed to us and in us.

We see that while the believer is more intent on trying to

discover the secret of true holiness from the divine side, he may be tolerating glaring faults obvious to all those around him. Because of the lack of perfect teachableness, he may remain ignorant of the graces and beauties of holiness by which the Father would have him make the doctrine of holiness attractive to others. He may seek to live a holy life without seeking a perfectly *blameless* life.

There are saints who are holy but hard, holy but distant, or holy but sharp in their judgments of others—holy in man's eyes, but also unloving and selfish. The half-heathen Samaritan, for instance, was more kind and self-sacrificing than the holy Levite and priest. Even though this may be true, it is not the teaching of Scripture that is at fault. In linking "holy" and "without blemish" (or without blame) so closely, the Holy Spirit leads us to seek for the embodiment of holiness as a spiritual power in the blamelessness of practice and of daily life. Let every believer who rejoices in God's declaration that he is holy in Christ seek also to perfect holiness and reach out after nothing less than to be "blameless."

We can see how this blamelessness is particularly related to our relationship with others when we see how it is linked with love: "May the Lord make your love increase and overflow for each other and for everyone else. . . . May he strengthen your hearts so that you will be blameless and holy" (1 Thessalonians 3:12–13). The holiness (the positive, hidden divine life principle) and the blamelessness (the external human life practice) both find their strength, by which we are to be established in them, in our abounding and ever-flowing love.

Holiness and loving-kindness should be inseparably linked in our minds, as should be their reality in our lives. We have seen by our study that love is the element by which holiness works itself out to those around us. If holiness is a divine fire, love is its flame. In God's children, true holiness is the same: the divine fire burns to bring into its own blessedness all that comes within its reach. When

Jesus sanctified himself that we might be sanctified in truth, it was love giving itself to death that the sinful might share in His holiness. Selfishness and holiness are irreconcilable. Ignorance may think of sanctity as a beautiful garment with which to adorn itself before God, while underneath selfish pride is saying, "I am holier than thou," and is quite content that others lack what it possesses. On the contrary, true holiness is the expulsion and the death of selfishness. Holiness takes possession of the heart and life to make them ministers of that fire of love that consumes itself, to reach out and purify and save others. Holiness is love. Abounding love is what Paul prays for as the condition of blameless holiness. It is as the Lord makes us increase and abound in love that He can establish our hearts without blame in holiness.

The Apostle speaks of a twofold love, "[love] for each other and for everyone else." Love to the brethren was what our Lord required as the salient mark of discipleship. And He prayed to the Father for it as the principal proof to the world of the truth of His divine mission. It is in a loving holiness that the unity of the body will be proved and promoted and prepared for the fuller workings of the Holy Spirit. In the letters to the Corinthians and the Galatians, division and distance between believers are named as sure proof of the life of self and the flesh. If we would be holy, we must begin by being very gentle and patient, forgiving and kind—generous in our relationships with all God's children. Study the divine image of the love that seeks not its own. Pray unceasingly that the Lord might cause us to abound in love toward one another. The holiest will be the humblest and most self-forgetting, the gentlest and most self-denying, the kindest and most thoughtful of others for Jesus' sake. "Therefore, as God's chosen people, holy and dearly loved, clothe yourselves with compassion, kindness, humility, gentleness and patience" (Colossians 3:12).

Love toward all men is the love proved in the course and

conduct of daily life. It is a love that not only avoids anger and evil temper and harsh judgments but also exhibits the more positive virtue of active devotion to the welfare and interests of all. Charitable love cares for bodies as well as souls: a love that not only is ready to help when called but that also gives itself up to self-denial and self-sacrifice to discover and relieve the needs of the most wretched and unworthy. It is a love that truly takes Christ's love—that allowed Him to leave heaven and choose the cross—as the only law and measure of its conduct, and makes everything subordinate to the Godlike blessedness of giving, of doing good, of embracing, and saving the needy and the lost. If we abound in this kind of love, we shall be blameless in holiness.

In Christ we are holy; of God we are in Christ, who is made unto us sanctification. In this faith Paul prays that the Lord Jesus may make us increase and abound in love. The Father is the fountain; Jesus Christ is the channel; the Holy Spirit is the living stream. And the Lord Jesus is our life, through the Spirit. By faith in Him, by abiding in Him and in His love, by allowing—in close union with Christ—the Spirit to shed abroad the love of God, we shall receive the answer to our prayers and shall by Him be established as blameless in holiness. Pray with a faith that changes into praise: Blessed be the Lord, who will make us increase and abound in love and will establish us in holiness before our God and Father at the coming of our Lord Jesus with His holy ones.

Most Gracious God and Father, again I thank you for that wondrous salvation, through sanctification of the Spirit, which has made us holy in Christ. I thank you that the Spirit can make us partakers of the life of Christ that we may be blameless in holiness. I thank you that the Lord himself makes us increase and abound in love and makes our hearts steadfast.

Blessed Lord and Savior, I come now to claim as my own all you promise to do for me. I am holy only in you. In you there is the power I need to abound in love. O Lord, my Lord, in whom the fullness of God's love abides and in whom I abide, cause me to abound in love. By the teaching of your Holy Spirit, lead me in all the steps of your self-denying love that I may be consumed with blessing others.

Let self perish before your presence, and establish my heart to live before you in blameless holiness. Preserve me unto your coming. Amen.

Personal Application

1. Let us pray very earnestly that our interest in the study of holiness may not be simply a thing of the intellect or the emotions but of the will and the life, seen of all men in our daily walk and conversation. "Abounding in love, blameless in holiness" finds favor with God and man.

2. "God is love"; creation is the outflow of love. Redemption is the sacrifice and the triumph of love, and holiness is its fire. The beauty of the life of Jesus is love. All we enjoy of the divine we owe to love. If we do not have love, our holiness is not God's holiness.

3. "[Love] is not self-seeking" (1 Corinthians 13:5). "Love never fails" (1 Corinthians 13:8). "Love is the fulfillment of the law" (Romans 13:10). "The greatest of these is love" (1 Corinthians 13:13). "The end of the commandment is love." To love God and man is to be holy. In the course of daily life, holiness will have its simple beginnings and its practice; in its highest attainment, holiness is love made perfect.

4. Faith has its worth from the love of God from which it draws and drinks and the love to God and man that streams out of it. Let us be strong in faith; then shall we abound in love.

5. "God has poured out his love into our hearts by the Holy Spirit, whom he has given us" (Romans 5:5). Let this be our confidence.

Chapter 26

Holiness and the Will of God

It is God's will that you should be sanctified.

1 Thessalonians 4:3

"Here I am, I have come to do your will.". . . by that will, we have been made holy through the sacrifice of the body of Jesus Christ once for all.

Hebrews 10:9–10

In the will of God we have the union of His wisdom and power. Wisdom decides and declares what is to be and power secures the performance. The declarative will is only one side; its complement, the executive will, is the living energy in which everything good has its origin and existence. So long as we only look at the will of God in the former light, as law, we feel it is a burden, because we do not have the power to perform it—it is too high for us. But when faith looks to the power that works in God's will and carries it out, then faith has the courage to accept and fulfill God's will because it knows God himself is working it out. The surrender in faith to the divine will as wisdom becomes the pathway to the experience of its power.

"He does as he pleases" (Daniel 4:35) is the expression not only of forced submission but of joyful expectation.

"It is God's will that you should be sanctified" (1 Thessalonians 4:3). Ordinarily, these words are simply taken to mean that sanctification is one among many other things that God has willed. There is some value in this thought in that God distinctly and definitely has willed your sanctification. We are "chosen . . . through the sanctifying work of the Spirit"(1 Peter 1:2) and "[chosen] to be holy" (Ephesians 1:4); the purpose of God's will from eternity, and His will now, is our sanctification. But think about God's will being a divine power that works out what His wisdom has chosen, and see how this truth will strengthen your faith that you should be holy. God not only wills it but will also work it out for all who do not resist but yield themselves to its power. Seek your sanctification not only as part of the will of God, as a declaration of what He wants you to be, but also as a revelation of what He surely will work out in you.

If our sanctification is God's will, our entrance into it will be the heartfelt acceptance of the will of God in all things. To be one with God's will is to be holy. Let him who would be holy take his place here and "stand firm in all the will of God" (Colossians 4:12). He will there meet God himself and be made partaker of His holiness because His will works out its purpose in power to each one who yields himself to it. Everything in a life of holiness depends upon our being in the right relationship to the will of God.

Many Christians think it is impossible to accept all the will of God, much less be one with it. They look upon God's will as a catalog of commands, and sometimes have found it extremely hard to obey even one of them, or to bear willingly some small disappointment. They imagine that they would need to be a hundredfold holier and stronger in grace before venturing to say that they accept *all* God's will. They cannot understand that the difficulty comes from their not occupying the right point of view. They think God's will is always at variance with their natural will, and that their natural will can never delight in God's will. They forget that the new creature in Christ has a renewed will. And this new will delights in the will of God because it is born of it. The new will sees the beauty and the glory of God's will and is in harmony with it. If they are indeed God's children, their very first impulse is to do the will of the Father in heaven. They have only to yield themselves heartily and wholly to this spirit of sonship, and not fear to accept God's will as their own.

The mistake they make is a very serious one. Instead of living by faith, they judge by feeling, in which the old nature speaks and rules. It tells them that God's will is a burden too hard to bear and that they never will have the strength to do it. Contrarily, faith reminds us that God is love and that His will is nothing but love revealed. It tells us that there is nothing more perfect or beautiful in heaven or earth than the will of God. It reminds us that at our conversion we already professed to accept God as Father and Lord. It assures us, above all, that if we will but trust ourselves to that will, it will fill our hearts and make us delight in it, and so become the power that enables us to do His will and to bear all joyfully. Faith reveals to us that the will of God is the power of His love working out its plan in divine beauty in each one who wholly yields to it.

How shall it be? Will we attempt to accept Christ as Savior without accepting His will? Will we profess to be the Father's children and spend our life debating how much of His will we will do? Shall we be content to go on from day to day with the painful consciousness that our will is not in harmony with God's? Or will we at once and forever give up our will for His—to that which He has already written on our hearts? This surrender is possible. It *can* be made. In a simple, definite transaction with God, we can say that we accept His holy will as ours. Faith knows that God will not pass by such a surrender unnoticed but will accept it. In the confidence that He takes us up into His heart and breathes His will into us—with the love and the power to perform it—let us enter into God's will and begin a new life, standing and abiding in the very center of His most holy will.

Such an acceptance of God's will prepares the believer, through the Holy Spirit, to recognize and know that will in whatever form it comes. The great difference between the carnal and the spiritual Christian is that the latter acknowledges God in whatever human appearance He manifests himself. When God comes in trials that can be traced to no hand but His, the spiritual Christian says, "Your will be done" (Matthew 26:42). When trials come, either through the weakness of others or through his own carelessness, when circumstances are unfavorable to his spiritual progress and temptations threaten to overcome him, he learns to see God first in everything and to say, "Your will be done." He knows that a child of God cannot possibly be found in any situation without the will of His heavenly Father, even when that will has been to leave him to his own willfulness for a time or to suffer the consequences of his own or others' sins. He sees this, and in accepting his circumstances as the will of God to prove him, he is in the right position for knowing and doing what is right. Seeing and honoring God's will in everything, he learns always to abide in that will.

He does so by doing that will. As his spiritual discernment grows to be able to say of whatever happens, "All this is from God" (2 Corinthians 5:18), so he grows too in wisdom and spiritual understanding to know the will of God as it is to be done. In the indications of conscience and of Providence, in the teaching of the Word and the Spirit, he learns to see how God's will has reference to every part and every duty of life, and it becomes his joy in all things to live "doing the will of God from [the] heart ... serving the Lord, not men" (Ephesians 6:6–7). "Wrestling in prayer ... that you may stand firm in all the will of God, mature and fully assured" (Colossians 4:12), he finds how blessedly the Father has accepted his surrender, and supplies all the light and strength that is needed that His will may be done by him on earth as it is in heaven.

Have you given yourself to this Holy God that He might make you holy? Have you accepted and entered into the good and perfect will of God? Are you living in it? The question is not whether when affliction comes you accept the inevitable and submit to a will you cannot resist, but whether you have chosen the will of God as your chief good and have taken the life principle of Christ to be yours: "I desire to do your will, O my God" (Psalm 40:8). This was the holiness of Christ, in which He sanctified himself and us by doing God's will—"in which will we have been sanctified." It is this will of God that is our sanctification.

The question is, do you truly want to be holy? to be wholly possessed of God? Here is the path: do not to be afraid or hold back. You have taken God to be your God; take His will to be your will. Think of the privilege, the blessedness, of having one will with God! Fear not to surrender yourself to it unreservedly. The will of God is in every part and in all its divine power your sanctification.

Blessed Father, I see that your will is my sanctification, and I will seek it. Graciously grant that by your Holy Spirit, which dwells in me, the glory of that will, and the blessedness of abiding in it, may be fully revealed to me. Teach me to know it as the will of Love, purposing always what is the very best and most blessed for your child. Teach me to know it as the will of Omnipotence, able to work out its counsel in me. Teach me to know it in Christ, fulfilled perfectly on my behalf. Teach me to know it as what the Spirit wills and works in each one who yields to Him.

O my Father, I acknowledge your claim to have your will alone done, and I am here for you to do with me as you please. With my whole heart I enter into your will, to be one with it forever. Your Holy Spirit can maintain this oneness without interruption. I trust you, my Father, step by step, to let the light of your will shine in my heart and on my path through that Spirit.

May this be the holiness by which I live, that I forget and lose myself in pleasing and honoring you. Amen.

Personal Application

1. Make it a study in meditation and prayer and worship to get a full impression of the majesty, the perfection, and the glory of the will of God, along with the privilege and possibility of living in it.

2. Study His will as the expression of an infinite love and fatherliness, its every manifestation full of loving-kindness. Providence is God's will; whatever happens, meet God in it in humble worship. Every precept is God's will; meet God in it with loving obedience. Every promise is God's will; meet God in it with complete trust. A life in the will of God is rest and strength and blessing.

3. Above all, do not forget to believe in its omnipotent power. He works all things after the counsel of His will: in nature and in those who resist Him, without their consent; in His children, according to their faith and as far as they will it. Do believe that the will of God will work out its counsel in you as you trust it to do so.

4. This will is infinite benevolence and beneficence revealed in the self-sacrifice of Jesus. Live for others so you can become an instrument for the divine will to use (Matthew 18:14; John 6:39–40). Yield yourselves to this redeeming will of God that it may take full possession and work out through you its saving purpose.

5. Christ is the embodiment of God's will: He is God's will done. Abide in Him by abiding in and doing heartily and always the will of God. A Christian is, like Christ, simply a person given up to the will of God.

Holiness and Service

If a man cleanses himself from the latter, he will be an instrument for noble purposes, made holy, useful to the Master and prepared to do any good work.

2 Timothy 2:21

A holy priesthood, offering spiritual sacrifices . . . a holy nation . . . that you may declare the praises of him who called you out of darkness into his wonderful light.

1 Peter 2:5, 9

Through all of Scripture we have seen that whatever God sanctifies is to be used in the service of His holiness. To the revelation of what He is: "I, the Lord, am holy" (Leviticus 20:26), God continually adds the declaration of what He does: "I am the Lord that makes holy." Holiness is a burning fire that extends itself, that seeks to consume what is unholy and to communicate its own blessedness to all that will receive it. Holiness and selfishness, holiness and inactivity, holiness and sloth, holiness and helplessness, are utterly incompatible.

What was revealed as holy in Scripture? The seventh day was made holy so that in it God might make His people holy. The tabernacle was holy, and was to serve as a dwelling place for the Holy

One, as the center from which His holiness might manifest itself to the people. The altar was most holy that it might sanctify the gifts laid upon it. The priests with their garments, the house with its furniture and vessels, the sacrifices and the blood—whatever bore the name "holy" had a use and a purpose. God said of Israel, whom He redeemed from Egypt that they might be a holy nation: "Let my people go, so that they may worship me" (Exodus 8:1). The holy angels, the holy prophets and apostles, the holy Scriptures—all bore the description as having been sanctified for the service of God. Our Lord speaks of himself as "the one whom the Father set apart as his very own and sent into the world" (John 10:36). And when He says, "I sanctify myself" (John 17:19), He adds at once the purpose: it is in the service of the Father and His redeemed ones "that they too may be truly sanctified" (John 17:19).

Is it possible that holiness and service would be cast aside now that God in Christ and in the Holy Spirit is accomplishing His purpose of gathering a people of saints ("holy ones made holy in Christ")? No! First we will see how essential they are to each other. Let us try to grasp the mutual relationship—we are made holy that we may serve. We can serve only as we are holy.

Holiness is essential to effectual service. In the Old Testament we see degrees of holiness, not only in the holy places but also in holy people. First it is seen in the nation, then the Levites, the priests, and the high priest. As in each succeeding stage the circle narrows and the service is more refined and distinct, so the holiness required is more refined and distinct. This is also true in this more spiritual dispensation: the more there is of holiness, the greater the fitness for service. The more there is of true holiness, the more there is of God, and the truer and deeper is the entrance He has had into the soul. The hold He has on the soul to use it in His service is more complete.

In the church of Christ there is a vast amount of work done that yields very little fruit. Many throw themselves into service without true holiness and with little of the Holy Spirit. They often work diligently, and as far as human influence is concerned, successfully. And yet true spiritual results are few. The Lord cannot work through these people because He does not rule in their inner life. They are comparative strangers to His personal indwelling and fellowship, to the rest that comes from His holy presence reigning and ruling in the heart. It has been rightly said that work in God's kingdom is the cure for spiritual poverty and disease; to some believers who had been seeking holiness apart from service, the call to work has been an unspeakable blessing. But to many it has been only a cover-up for their lack of heart holiness and fellowship with the living God. They have thrown themselves into the work more earnestly than ever and yet do not have in their hearts the rest and refreshing witness that their work is acceptable to God.

"In a large house there are articles not only of gold and silver, but also of wood and clay; some are for noble purposes and some for ignoble. If a man cleanses himself from the latter, he will be an instrument for noble purposes, made holy, useful to the Master and prepared to do any good work" (2 Timothy 2:20–21). You cannot have the law of service more clearly or beautifully laid down. A vessel of honor, one whom the King will delight to honor, must be a vessel cleansed from all defilement of flesh and spirit. Only then can it be a sanctified vessel, possessed and indwelt by God's Holy Spirit. So it becomes meet for the Master's use. He can use it, work in it, and wield it. And so, clean and holy, yielded into the Master's hands, we are divinely prepared for every good work. Holiness is essential to service. If our service is to be acceptable to God and effectual in its work with souls, and is to be a joy and strength to us, we must be holy. The will of God must first live in us if it is to be done by us.

How many faithful workers in the church mourn the lack of

power, long and pray for it, and yet do not obtain it. They have spent their strength in the outer court of work and service and have nothing left for the inner life of fellowship and faith. They have never understood that only as the Master gains possession of them, as they are at the disposal of the Holy Spirit, can He use them. And so they long and cry for a baptism of power, forgetting that the way to have it is to live in obedience to God and to allow the Holy Spirit to dwell within, as in His temple, ruling all. Again, holiness is essential to effectual service.

Service is *equally* essential to true holiness. Holiness is an intense energy of desire and self-sacrifice to make others partakers of its own purity and perfection. Christ sacrificed himself. Of what did that sacrifice consist and what was its aim? He sanctified himself that we might be sanctified. A holiness that is selfish is a delusion. True holiness, God's holiness in us, works itself out in love, in seeking and loving the unholy, that they may become holy too. Self-sacrificing love is the very essence of holiness. The Holy One of Israel is its Redeemer. The Holy One of God is the dying Savior. The Holy Spirit of God makes holy. There is no holiness in God except that which is actively engaged in loving and saving and blessing. It must be so in us too. Every thought of holiness, every act of faith or prayer, every effort in pursuit of it must be animated by the desire and the surrender of its object. Let your whole life be one distinctly and definitely surrendered to God for His use and service. Your circumstances may appear to be unfavorable. God may appear to keep the door closed against your working for Him in the way you would wish; your sense of unfitness may be painful. Even so, let the matter be settled between God and your soul: your longing for holiness is so that you may be better fitted for His use, and what He has given you of His holiness in Christ and the Spirit is all at His disposal. Be ready for Him to use you, live out in a daily life of humble, self-denying, loving service to others what grace you have received. You will find that in the union and interchange of worship and work God's holiness will rest upon you.

The Father sanctified the Son, and sent him into the world. The world is the place for the one who is sanctified to be its light, its salt, its life. We are sanctified in Christ Jesus and sent into the world. Let us not be afraid to accept our position, our double position—in the world with its sin and sorrow, with its myriad needs touching us at every turn and its millions of souls all waiting for us—and in Christ. For the sake of that world we have been sanctified in Christ; we are holy in Christ; we have the spirit of sanctification dwelling in us. As salt in a sinful world, let us give ourselves to our holy calling. Let us come nearer and nearer to God who has called us. Let us take root deeper and deeper in Christ our sanctification—in whom we are of God. Let us enter more firmly and more fully into that faith in Him in whom we are, so that our whole life will be covered and taken up in His. Let us beseech the Father to teach us that His Holy Spirit dwells in us every moment, making Christ with His holiness our home, our abode, our sure defense, and our infinite supply. As He that has called us is holy, let us be holy in His Son, through His Spirit, and the fire of His holy love will work through us its work of judging and condemning, of saving and sanctifying. A sanctified soul God will use to save.

Blessed Master, I thank you for being reminded again of the purpose of your redeeming love. You gave yourself that you might cleanse for yourself a people of your own, zealous in good works. You would make of each of us a vessel of honor, cleansed and sanctified, meet for your use, and prepared for every good work.

Blessed Lord, write the lessons of your Word deep on my heart. Teach your people that if we would work for you, if we would have you work in us and use us, we must be holy—holy as God is holy. And that if we would be holy, we must serve you. It is your own Spirit by which you sanctify us to use us, and in using us you sanctify us. To be entirely possessed of you is both the path to sanctification and to service.

Most Holy Savior, we are in you as our sanctification: in you we would abide. In the rest of a faith that trusts you for all, in the power of a surrender that would have no will but yours, in a love that would lose itself to be wholly yours, blessed Jesus, we will abide. In you we are holy: in you we shall bear fruit.

Be pleased to perfect your own work in us! Amen.

Personal Application

1. It is difficult to make it clear in words how growth in holiness will simply reveal itself as an increasing simplicity and self-forgetfulness, accompanied by the restful and blessed assurance that God has complete possession of us and will use us. We pass from the stage in which work presses as an obligation; it becomes the joy of fruit-bearing: faith's assurance that He is working out His will through us.

2. It has sometimes been said that people might be better employed in working for God than in attending holiness conventions. This is surely a misunderstanding. It was before the throne of the Thrice-Holy One, and as he heard the seraphim sing of God's holiness, that the prophet said, "Here am I, send me." Just as the missions of Moses, of Isaiah, and of the Son, whom the Father sanctified and sent, each had their origin in the revelation of God's holiness, so our missions will receive new power as they are more directly born out of worship of God as the Holy One and baptized into the Spirit of holiness.

3. Let every worker take time to hear God's double call. If you would work, you must be holy. If you would be holy, give yourself to God to use in His work.

4. Note the connection between "sanctified" and "meet for the Master's use." True holiness is being possessed of God; true

service is being used of God. There is so much service in which we are the chief agents, and we only ask God to help and to bless us. True service is being yielded up to the Master for Him to use. Then the Holy Spirit is the agent and we are the instruments of His will. Such service is holiness.

5. "I sanctify myself, that they too may be truly sanctified": an interest in helping others is the root principle of all true holiness.

Chapter 28

The Way Into the Holiest

Therefore, brothers, since we have confidence to enter the Most Holy Place by the blood of Jesus, by a new and living way opened for us through the curtain, that is, his body, and since we have a great priest over the house of God, let us draw near to God with a sincere heart in full assurance of faith.

Hebrews 10:19–22

When the high priest once a year entered into the second tabernacle within the veil, we are told in Hebrews, "The Holy Spirit was showing by this that the way into the Most Holy Place had not yet been disclosed" (Hebrews 9:8). When Christ died, the veil was rent. All who were serving in the holy place had free access at once into the most holy. The way into the holiest of all was opened up. When the epistle passes over to its practical application (Hebrews 10:19), all its teaching is summed up in the words "Therefore, brothers, since we have confidence to enter the Most Holy Place . . . let us draw near." Christ's redemption has opened the way to the holiest of all: our acceptance of it must lead to nothing less than our drawing near and entering in. The text suggests four thoughts in regard to the place of access, the right of access, the way of access, and the power of access.

The place of access. To what place are we invited to draw near? "Therefore, brothers, since we have confidence to enter the Most Holy Place. . . ." The priests in Israel might enter the holy place, but were always excluded from the holiest, God's immediate presence. The rent veil proclaimed liberty of access into that presence. It is there that believers as a royal priesthood are now to live and walk. Within the veil, in the very holiest of all, in the heavenlies, where God dwells, in His very presence—this is to be our abode—our home. Some say "Let us draw near" refers to prayer, and that in our special approach to God in acts of worship we enter the holiest. As great as the privilege of prayer is, God means something infinitely greater for us. We are to draw near and dwell—live our life and do our work—always within the sphere, the atmosphere, of the inner sanctuary. It is God's presence that makes any place the holiest of all, and it is in this presence we are to abide. There is not a single moment of the day, not a circumstance or surrounding that can block the believer's continual dwelling in the secret place of the Most High. As by faith we enter into the completeness of our reconciliation with God and the reality of our oneness with Christ, and as we, abiding in Christ, yield to the Holy Spirit to reveal the presence of the Holy One, the holiest of all is around us and in us. With an uninterrupted access we may draw near.

The right of access. Is this right simply an ideal? Or can it be a reality, an experience in daily life to those who know how sinful their nature is? Blessed be God, it is possible, because our right of access rests not in what *we* are but in the blood of Jesus. "Therefore, brothers, since we have confidence to enter the Most Holy Place by the blood of Jesus . . . let us draw near." In the Passover we saw how redemption and the holiness it aimed at were dependent on the blood. In the sanctuary, God's dwelling, we know how in each part—the court, the holy place, the most holy—the sprinkling of blood was what alone secured access to God. And now that the blood of Jesus has been shed, what divine power, what intense reality, what everlasting efficacy we have in gaining access into the holiest of all, the most holy of God's heart and His love. We are brought nigh by the blood; we have boldness to enter by the blood. "The worshipers would have been cleansed once for all, and would no longer have felt guilty for their sins" (Hebrews 10:2). Walking in the light, the blood of Jesus cleanses in the power of an endless life, with a cleansing that never ceases. No consciousness of unworthiness or remaining sinfulness needs to hinder the boldness of access. The liberty to draw near rests in the never-failing, ever-acting, ever-living efficacy of the precious blood. It is possible for a believer to dwell in the holiest of all.

The way of access. It is often thought that the new and living way, dedicated for us by Jesus, is simply boldness through His blood. The words mean a great deal more. "Since we have confidence . . . by the blood of Jesus . . . let us draw near" by the way which he dedicated for us. He opened for us a way to walk in, as He walked in it, "a new and living way . . . through the curtain, that is, his body." The way in which Christ walked when He shed His blood is the very same in which we must walk. That way is the way of the cross. There must not only be faith in Christ's sacrifice but also fellowship with Him in it. That way led to the rending of the veil of the flesh, and so through the rent veil, into the presence of God. And was the veil of Christ's holy flesh rent that the veil of our sinful flesh might be spared? No. He meant for us to walk in the same way He did, following closely after Him. He dedicated for us a new and living way through the veil, that is, His flesh. As we go in through the rent veil of His flesh, we find in it at once the need and the power for our flesh to be rent too: following Jesus always means conformity to Him. It is Jesus with the rent flesh, in whom we are, in whom we walk. There is no way to God but through the rending of the flesh. In acceptance of Christ's life and death by faith as the power that works in us, in the power of the Spirit that makes us truly one with Christ, we all follow Christ as He passes on through the rent veil, that is, His flesh, and we become partakers with Him of His crucifixion and death. The way of the cross, by which I have been crucified, is the way through the rent veil. Man's destiny, fellowship with God in the power of the Holy Spirit, is only reached through the sacrifice of the flesh.

Here we find the solution of a great mystery—why so many Christians stand far off and never enter this holiest of all; why the holiness of God's presence is so little seen in them. They thought that it was only in Christ that the flesh needed to be rent and not in themselves. They thought that the liberty they had in the blood was the new and living way. They didn't know that the way into true and full holiness, into the holiest of all—full entrance into the fellowship of the holiness of the Great High Priest—was only to be reached through the rent veil of the flesh, through conformity to the death of Jesus. This is the way that He dedicated for us. He is the way. Into His self-denial, His self-sacrifice, His crucifixion, He takes up all who long to be holy with His holiness, holy as He is holy.

The power of access. Does anyone shrink back from entering the very holiest for fear of this rending of the flesh because he doubts whether he could bear it, whether he could walk in such a path? Let him listen once more: "And since we have a great priest over the house of God, let us draw near." We have not only the holiest of all inviting us, and the blood giving us boldness, and the way through the rent veil consecrated for us, but we have the High Priest over the house of God, the blessed living Savior, to draw, to help, and to welcome us. He is our Aaron. On His heart we see our name, because He only lives to think of us and pray for us. On His forehead we see God's name, "Holy to the Lord" (Exodus 28:36), because in His holiness the sins of our best intentions are covered. In Him we are accepted and sanctified; God receives us as holy ones. In the power of His love and His Spirit, in the power of the Holy One, in the joy of drawing nearer to Him and being drawn by Him, we gladly accept the way He has dedicated and walk in His holy footsteps of self-denial and self-sacrifice. We see how the flesh is the veil that separates from the Holy One who is Spirit, and it becomes an unceasing and most fervent prayer that the crucifixion of the flesh may, in the power of the Holy Spirit, be in us a blessed reality. With the glory of the holiest of all shining out on us through the opened veil, and the precious blood speaking loudly of boldness of access, the High Priest beckoning us with His loving presence to draw near and be blessed—we dare no longer fear, but choose the way of the rent veil as the path we love to tread, and give ourselves to enter in and dwell within the veil, in the very holiest of all.

Our life here will be the foretaste of the glory that is promised in four great thoughts of our text: "These are they who have come out of the great tribulation" (Revelation 7:14), that is, by the way of the rent flesh; "they have washed their robes and made them white in the blood of the Lamb" (Revelation 7:14), their boldness through the blood; therefore, "they are before the throne of God" (Revelation 7:15), their dwelling in the holiest of all; "For the Lamb at the center of the throne will be their shepherd" (Revelation 7:17)—the Great Priest still the Shepherd, Jesus himself their all in all.

Do you see what holiness is and how it is to be found? It is not something formed in you. It is not something put on you from without. Holiness is the presence of God resting on you. Holiness comes as you consciously abide in that presence, doing all your work and living all your life as a sacrifice to Him, acceptable through Jesus Christ, sanctified by the Holy Spirit, not harboring fear that this life is not for you! Look to Jesus. Having a Great High Priest over the house of God, let us draw near. Be occupied with Jesus. Our Brother is in charge of the temple; He has liberty to show us around, to lead us into the secret of the Father's presence. The entire management of the temple has been given into His hands with this very purpose, that all the weak and faint and doubting might come with confidence. Trust yourself to Jesus, to His leading and His keeping. Only trust Jesus, God's Holy One; it is His delight to reveal to you what He has purchased with His blood. Trust Him to teach you the ordinance of the sanctuary. "You will know how people ought to conduct themselves in God's household" (1 Timothy 3:15). Having a Great High Priest, let us enter in and let us dwell in the holiest of all. In the power of the blood, in the power of the new and living way, in the power of the living Jesus, let the holiest of all, the presence of God, be the home of your soul. You are holy in Christ; in Christ you are in God's holy presence and love; remain there.

Most Holy God, how I praise you for the liberty to enter into the holiest of all and dwell there. And for the precious blood that brings us near. For the new and living way through the rent veil of the flesh, in which our flesh has also been crucified, and for the Great High Priest over the house of God, our living Lord Jesus, with whom and in whom we appear before you. Glory be to your holy name for this wonderful and most complete redemption.

I ask you, O God, to give all your children a true concept of the reality that we may live each day, spend our whole life, within the veil, in your own immediate presence. Give us the spirit of revelation, I pray, that we may see how the glory of your presence streams forth through the rent veil from the most holy into the holy place. Show us how, in the pouring out of the Holy Spirit, the kingdom of heaven has come to earth, and how all who yield themselves to that Spirit may know that in Christ they are indeed near to you. O Blessed Father, let your Spirit teach us that this indeed is the holy life: a life in Christ the Holy One, always in the light and presence of your Holy Majesty.

I draw near to you. In the power of the Holy Spirit I enter in. I am now in the holiest of all. And here I would abide in Jesus, my Great High Priest—here, in the holiest of all. Amen.

Personal Application

1. To abide in Christ is to dwell in the holiest of all. Christ is not only the sacrifice, and the way, and the Great High Priest, but also the temple: The Lamb is the temple. As the Holy Spirit reveals my union to Christ more clearly, my heart and will are lost in Him and I dwell in the holy presence, the holiest of all. You are holy in Christ—draw near, enter in with boldness, and take possession; have no home but in the holiest of all.

2. "Christ loved the church and gave himself up for her to make her holy" (Ephesians 5:25–26). He gave himself! Have you caught the force of that word? Because He would have no one else do it, because none could do it; to sanctify His church, He gave *himself.* And so it is His own special beloved work to sanctify the church He loved. Accept His work for you. He can and will make you holy that He may present you to himself glorious, without spot or wrinkle. Let that word *himself* live in you. The whole life and walk in the house of God is in His charge. Having a Great High Priest, let us draw near.

3. This entrance into the holiest of all—an ever-fresh and ever-deeper entrance—is, at the same time, a blessed resting in the Father's presence. Faith in the blood, following in the way of the rent flesh, and fellowship with the living Jesus are the three chief steps.

4. Enter into the holiest of all and dwell there. It will enter into you, transform you, and dwell in you. Your heart will become a holy place for His dwelling.

5. Have we not at times been lifted by thought or will, or in the fellowship of the saints into what seemed the holiest of all, but suddenly felt that the flesh had entered too? This can happen

when we have not entered by the new way of life—the way through death to life, the way of the rent veil of the flesh. Teach us, Lord, what this means; show us the way to the holiest place.

6. Let me remember that my access into the holiest is as a priest. Let me dwell before the Lord all the day as an intercessor, offering unceasing supplication that is acceptable in Christ. May God's church be like her of whom it is written, "She never left the temple but worshiped night and day, fasting and praying" (Luke 2:37). It is for this that we have access to the holiest of all.

—— *Chapter 29* ——

Holiness and Chastisement

*But God disciplines us for our good, that we may share in his
holiness. . . . without holiness no one will see the Lord.*

Hebrews 12:10, 14

Perhaps no part of God's Word sheds more divine light on suffering
than the epistle to the Hebrews. This is because it teaches us what
suffering was to the Son of God. It perfected His humanity and fitted Him for His work as the compassionate High Priest. It proved
that He who had fulfilled God's will in suffering obedience was indeed worthy to be its executor in glory and to sit down on the right
hand of the Majesty on high. "In bringing many sons to glory, it was
fitting that God . . . should make the author of their salvation perfect
through suffering" (Hebrews 2:10). "Although he was a son, he
learned obedience from what he suffered and, once made perfect,
he became the source of eternal salvation for all who obey him"
(Hebrews 5:8–9). As He said himself about His suffering, "I sanctify
myself" (John 17:19), so we see here that His sufferings were indeed
to Him the pathway to perfection and holiness.

What Christ was and won was all for us. And it is the power of the new life that comes from Him to us. In the light of His example, we can prove that suffering is to God's child the token of the Father's love and the channel of His richest blessing. To such faith the apparent mystery of suffering is seen to be nothing but a divine need—the light affliction that works out the exceeding weight of glory. We agree not only to what is written, "It was fitting that God . . . should make the author of their salvation perfect through suffering," but we understand somewhat how divinely fitting and right it is that we too should be sanctified by suffering.

"God disciplines us for our good, that we may share in his holiness." Of all the precious words Holy Scripture has for the sorrowful, there is hardly one equal to this in leading us more directly and more deeply into the fullness of blessing that suffering is meant to bring. It is His holiness, God's own holiness, of which we are to partake. The epistle had explained clearly about our sanctification from its divine side, as worked out for us and formed in us by Jesus himself. "Both the one who makes men holy and those who are made holy are of the same family" (Hebrews 2:11). We have been sanctified by the one offering of Christ. In our text we have the other side, the progressive work by which we are to accept personally, and voluntarily appropriate, this divine holiness. What is this progressive work? There is much in us that clashes with God's will, and that must be discovered and broken down before we can understand what it is to give up our will and delight in God's. Only a personal experience and fellowship of suffering can lead to the full appreciation of what Jesus bore and did for us. Also, there must be the full personal entrance into the satisfaction with the love of God as our sufficient portion. Seeing these things, it is clear that chastisement and suffering are indispensable elements in God's work of making us holy. In these three aspects we will see how what the Son needed is what we need, how what was of such unspeakable value to the Son will be no less rich to us in blessing.

Chastisement leads us to the acceptance of God's will. We have seen how God's will is our sanctification; how it is in the will of God that Christ has sanctified us; and more, how He found the power to sanctify us in sanctifying himself by the entire surrender of His will to God. His "desire to do [God's] will" (Psalm 40:8) derived its value from His continual "not my will." When God comes with chastisement or suffering, His first object is to ask for and accomplish in us union with His own blessed will, that through it we may have union with Him and His love. He chooses one single point in which His will crosses our most cherished affection or desire and asks the surrender of what we will to what He wills. When this is done willingly and lovingly, He leads us on to see how that individual sacrifice is based on a principle—that in everything His will is to be our one desire. Happy is the soul to whom affliction is not a series of single acts—of conflict and then submission to His will—but an entrance into the school where we prove and approve all the good, perfect, and acceptable will of God.

Sometimes it is difficult to see the blessing in affliction, even to God's children. Affliction by nature stirs up opposition to God's will because a loss of peace and happiness has been suffered. But in spite of an initial negative response, the affliction is working out God's purposes: "To humble [us] and to test [us] in order to know what was in [our] heart" (Deuteronomy 8:2) is still His object in leading us into the wilderness. To a great extent we are not aware that the practice of our Christianity is often selfish and superficial. When we accept the teaching of chastisement in unmasking the self-will and love of the world that still prevails, we have learned one of its first and most necessary lessons.

This lesson is especially difficult when the trial does not come directly from God but through men or circumstances. In looking at second causes and in seeking for their removal, in the feeling of indignation or grief, we often forget to see God's will in everything

His providence allows. And as long as we do so, the chastisement is fruitless and perhaps only hardens the heart.

If, in our study of the pathway of holiness, there has been awakened in us the desire to accept, adore, and stand complete in all the will of God, let us first seek to recognize that will in everything that comes to or upon us. The sin of the one who troubles us is not God's will, but it is God's will that we should be in that position of difficulty to be tried and tested. Let our first thoughts be: "This position of difficulty is my Father's will for me. I accept that will as my place where He sees fit to try me." Such acceptance of the trial is the way to turn it into blessing. It will lead on to an understanding and more constant abiding in all the will of God.

Chastisement leads to the fellowship of God's Son. The will of God outside of Christ is a law we cannot fulfill. The will of God in Christ is a life that fills us. He came in the name of our fallen humanity and accepted all God's will as it rested on us, both in the demands of the law and in the consequences that sin brought upon man. He gave himself entirely to God's will, whatever it cost Him. And so He paved a way for us through suffering, not only through it in the sense of getting past it and out of it, but because of it, leading us on into the love and glory of the Father. And it is in the power that Christ gives in fellowship with himself that we too can love the way of the cross as the best and most blessed way to the crown. Scripture says that the will of God is our sanctification and also that Christ is our sanctification. Only in Christ do we have the power to love and rejoice in the will of God. In Him we have the power. He became our sanctification once and for all time by delighting to do that will. He becomes our sanctification in personal experience by teaching us to delight to do that will. He learned to do it, and He could not become perfect in doing it other than by suffering. In suffering He draws near; He makes our suffering the fellowship of His suffering, and in it makes himself—who was perfected through suffering—our sanctification.

All you who suffer, whom the Father is chastening, come and see Jesus' suffering, giving up His will, being made perfect, sanctifying himself. His suffering is the secret of His holiness, of His glory, and of His life. Will you thank God for anything that can admit you into closer fellowship with your blessed Lord? Shall we not accept every trial, great or small, as the call of His love to be one with Him in living only for God's will? This is holiness—to be one with Jesus as He does the will of God, to abide in Jesus who was made perfect through suffering.

Chastisement leads to the enjoyment of God's love. Many a father has been surprised at his first experience of a child, after being punished in love, clinging to him even more tenderly than before. In the same way, those who live at a distance from their Father find that the misery in this world appears to be the one thing that shakes their faith in God's love, where in reality it is through suffering that God's children learn to know the reality of that love. Chastening is distinctly a father's prerogative; it leads so directly to the admission that it was needed and that it was done in love. Also, it awakens powerfully the longing for pardon and comfort and deliverance. Strange though this may seem, it does indeed become one of the surest guides into the deeper experience of the divine love. Chastening is the school in which the blessed lesson is learned that the will of God is love, and that holiness is the fire of love, consuming that it may purify, destroying the dross only that it may assimilate into its own perfect purity all that yields itself to the wondrous change.

"We know and rely on the love God has for us. God is love. Whoever lives in love lives in God, and God in him" (1 John 4:16). Man's destiny is fellowship with God and an indwelling of love. It is only by faith that this love of God can be known. Faith can grow only by being exercised, and thrive only under trial. When visible things fail, faith's energy is motivated to yield itself to be possessed by the invisible, by the divine. Chastisement is one of faith's chosen attendants, to nourish it and lead it deeper into the love of God. This is the new and living way, the way of the rent flesh in fellowship with Jesus leading up into the holiest of all. There it is seen how the justice that will not spare the child and the love that sustains and sanctifies it are one in the holiness of God.

You who are chastened, who are especially being led in the way that goes through the rent veil of the flesh, you have boldness to enter in. Draw near; come and dwell in the holiest of all. Make your abode there. There you are made partakers of His holiness. Chastisement is bringing your heart into unity with God's will, God's Son, God's love. Abide in God's will. Abide in God's Son. Abide in God's love. Dwell within the veil, in the holiest of all.

Most Holy God! Once again I bless you for the wonderful revelation of your holiness. Not only have I heard you say, "I am holy," but you have invited me to fellowship with yourself: "Be holy, as I am holy." Blessed be your name! I have heard also: "I make holy," your word of promise, pledging your own power to work out the purpose of your love. I thank you for what you have revealed in your Son, by your Spirit, in your Word, of the path of holiness. But how shall I bless you for the lesson of this day, that there is not a loss or sorrow, not a pain or care, not a temptation or trial, but that your love also means it and makes it to be a help in working out the holiness of your people. Through each you draw to yourself that they may taste how, in accepting your will of love, there is blessing and deliverance.

Blessed Father, you know how often I have looked upon the circumstances and the difficulties of this life as hindrances. Now in the light of your holy purpose to make us partakers of your holiness and in view of your will and your love, I acknowledge my circumstances and even the difficulties of this life to be helps to me. Let, above all, the path of your blessed Son—proving how suffering is the discipline of a Father's love, surrender the secret of holiness, and sacrifice the entrance to the holiest of all—be so revealed that in the power of His Spirit and His grace that path may become mine. Let even the slightest chastening be from your own hand, making me a partaker of your holiness. Amen.

Personal Application

1. How wonderful is the revelation in the epistle to the Hebrews of the holiness and the holy-making power of suffering as seen in the Son of God. "He learned obedience from what he suffered" (Hebrews 5:8). "It was fitting that God ... should make the author of their salvation perfect through suffering. Both the one who makes men holy and those who are made holy are of the same family" (Hebrews 2:10–11). "He himself suffered ... he is able to help" (Hebrews 2:18). "We see Jesus ... now crowned with glory and honor" (Hebrews 2:9). Suffering is the way of the rent veil, the new and living way Jesus walked in and opened for us. Let all sufferers study this. Let all who are "holy in Christ" here learn to know the Christ in whom they are holy, and the way in which He sanctified himself and sanctifies us.

2. If we begin by realizing the sympathy of Jesus with us in our suffering, it will lead us on higher: sympathy with Jesus in His suffering, fellowship with Him to suffer even as He did.

3. Let suffering and holiness be inseparably linked, as in God's mind and in Christ's person, so in your life through the Spirit. It became God to make him perfect through suffering; for both he that sanctifies and they who are sanctified are all one. Let every trial, small or great, be seen as the touch of God's hand, laying hold on you, leading you to holiness.

4. "Rejoice that you participate in the sufferings of Christ ... for the Spirit of glory and of God rests on you" (1 Peter 4:13–14).

Chapter 30

The Unction From the Holy One

*But you have an anointing from the Holy One, and all of you
know the truth. . . . As for you, the anointing you received from
him remains in you, and you do not need anyone to teach you.
But as his anointing teaches you about all things and as that
anointing is real, not counterfeit—just as it has
taught you, remain in him.*

1 John 2:20, 27

In the revelation by Moses of God's holiness and His way of making holy, the priests, and especially the high priests, were the chief expressions of God's holiness in man. In the priests themselves, the holy anointing oil was the one symbol of the grace that made holy. Moses was to make a holy anointing oil: "And take . . . some of the anointing oil and sprinkle it on Aaron . . . and on his sons. . . . Then he and his sons . . . will be consecrated. . . . It will be the sacred anointing oil. Do not pour it on men's bodies and do not make any oil with the same formula. It is sacred, and you are to consider it sacred" (Exodus 29:21; 30:25, 32). With this the priests, and especially the high priests, were to be anointed and consecrated. "The high priest, the one among his brothers who has had the anointing oil poured on his head. . . . [He must not] leave the sanctuary of his God or desecrate it, because he has been dedicated by the anointing oil of his God" (Leviticus 21:10, 12). And even so it is said of David, as a type of the Messiah, "Our king [belongs] to the Holy One of Israel. . . . I have found David my servant; with my sacred oil I have anointed him" (Psalms 89:18, 20).

We know how the Hebrew name *Messiah*, and the Greek *Christ*, has reference to this. In the passage just quoted, the Hebrew is "With my sacred oil I have 'messiahed' him." And so in a passage like Acts 10:38: "God 'christed' Jesus of Nazareth with the Holy Spirit and power." Psalm 45:7: "God has set you above your companions by 'messiahing' you with the oil of joy." Hebrews 1:9: "Your God has set you above your companions by 'christing' you with the oil of joy." And so we are called Christians because we are fellow partakers with Him of His "christing," or His anointing. This is the anointing of which John speaks, the "chrisma" or "christing" of the Holy One. The Holy Spirit is the holy anointing that every believer receives. What God did to His Son to make Him the Christ, He does to us to make us Christians. "You have an anointing from the Holy One."

1. *"You have an anointing from the Holy One."* It is as the Holy One that the Father gives the anointing. The oil He uses to anoint is called the oil of holiness, the Holy Spirit. Holiness is indeed a divine ointment. Just as there is nothing so subtle and penetrating as the odor of the ointment that fills a house, so holiness is an indescribable, all-pervading breath of heavenliness that pervades the man on whom the anointing rests. Holiness does not consist in certain actions: this is righteousness. Rather, holiness is the unseen and yet obvious presence of the Holy One resting on His anointed. The anointing is received directly from the Holy One, or only in the abiding fellowship with Him in Christ, who is the Holy One of God.

Who receives it? Only he who has given himself completely to be holy as God is holy. The priest, who was separated to be holy to the Lord, received the anointing; upon other men's flesh it was not to be poured. How many would gladly have the precious ointment, even for the sake of its perfume, for themselves! But only he who is wholly consecrated to the service of the Holy One, to the work of the sanctuary, may receive it. If anyone had said, "I would be glad to have the anointing, but not so that I am made a priest; I am not ready to always be at the beck and call of sinners seeking their God," he could have no share in it. Holiness is the energy that lives to make holy and in so doing to bless. The anointing of the Holy One is for the priest, the servant of God Most High. Only in the intensity of a soul truly awakened and given up to God's glory, God's kingdom, and God's work, does holiness become a reality. The holy garments were prepared only for the priests and their service. In all our seeking after holiness, let us remember this. As we are careful of the error of thinking that any work for Christ will make us holy, let us also look out for the other error: the straining after holiness without work. The priest who is set apart for the service of the holy place and the Holy One, and the believer who is ready to live and die that the holiness of God may triumph among men around him, are the ones who will receive the anointing.

2. *"His anointing teaches you."* The new man is created in knowledge as well as in righteousness and holiness. Christ is made to us wisdom as well as righteousness and sanctification. God's service and our holiness are above all to be free and full, an intelligent and willing approval of His blessed will. And so the anointing, to fit us for the service of the sanctuary, teaches us to know all things. Just as the perfume of the ointment is a subtle essence, not visible or tangible, only perceptible by smell, so the spiritual faculty that the anointing gives is the subtlest there can be. It teaches us by a divine instinct; by it the anointed one recognizes what has the heavenly

fragrance and what is of earth. It is the anointing that makes the Word and the name of Jesus in the Word to be as ointment poured forth.

The great mark of the anointing is teachableness. It is the great mark of Christ, the Holy One of God, the Anointed One, that He listens: "The words I say to you are not just my own" (John 14:10). And so it is of the Holy Spirit: "He will not speak on his own; he will speak only what he hears" (John 16:13). It cannot be otherwise: one anointed with the anointing of this Christ, with this Holy Spirit, will be teachable, will listen so he can be taught. His anointing teaches. You do not need anyone to teach you. But his anointing teaches you about all things. They shall be all taught of God. This includes every believer. The secret of true holiness is a very direct and personal relationship with the Holy One. All the teaching through the Word or man is made entirely dependent on and subordinate to the personal teaching of the Holy Spirit. The teaching comes through the anointing. Not in the thoughts or feelings, but in that all-pervading fragrance that comes from the fresh oil having penetrated the whole inner man.

3. *"The anointing you received from him remains in you."* In the spiritual life it is of deep importance always to maintain harmony between the objective and the subjective: God in Christ above me, God by the Spirit within me. In us not as a location, but in us as one with us, entering into the most secret part of our being and pervading all, dwelling in our very body, the anointing remains in us, forming part of our essential being. And this is only to the degree that we know it and yield ourselves to it, as we wait and are quiet to let the secret fragrance permeate our whole being. And this will not be an interrupted, broken experience, but one that is continuous and unvarying. Above circumstances and feelings, the anointing remains. Not, indeed, as a fixed state or as something in our own possession, but according to the law of the new life, in the

dependence of faith on the Holy One and in the fellowship of Jesus. I am anointed with fresh oil—this is the objective side. Every morning the believer waits for the renewal of the divine gift from the Father. "The anointing . . . remains in you"—this is the subjective side. The holy life, the life of faith and fellowship and anointing, is always, from moment to moment, a spiritual reality.

4. *"Just as it has taught you, remain in him."* Here we have again the Holy Trinity: the Holy One, from whom the holy anointing comes; the Holy Spirit, who is himself the anointing; and Christ, the Holy One of God, in whom the anointing teaches us to abide. In Christ, the unseen holiness of God was set before us and brought near; it became human, vested in a human nature that it might be communicated to us. Within us the Holy Spirit dwells and works, drawing us out to Christ, uniting us in heart and will to Him, and then revealing Him and forming Him within us so that His likeness and mind are a part of us. It is thus we abide in Christ: the holy anointing of the Holy One teaches us this. It is this that is the test of the true anointing: abiding in Christ, as He meant it to be, becomes truth in us. The life of holiness comes through the Trinity: first, the Father, who makes holy; second, the Son, His Holy One in whom we are; and third, the Holy Spirit, who dwells in us and through whom we abide in Christ and Christ in us.

Let us study the divine anointing. It is God's way of making us partakers of holiness in Christ. The anointing, received of Him day by day, abiding in us, teaching us all things, especially teaches us to abide in Christ. Its subtle, all-pervading power must go through our whole life. The odor of the ointment must fill the house. The anointing that abides makes abiding in Christ a reality and a certainty. To His holy name be all the praise!

O Holy One, I come to you now for renewed anointing. O Father, this is the one gift your child may most surely count on—the gift of your Holy Spirit. Enable me now to sing, "You anointed my head; I am anointed with fresh oil."

I confess with shame that your Spirit has been sorely grieved and dishonored. How often the flesh has usurped His place in your worship! How much the human will has sought to do His work! O my Father, let your light shine through me to convince me deeply of this. Let your judgment come on all that there is of human willing and doing.

Grant me, blessed Father, according to the riches of your glory, to be strengthened now with might by your Spirit in the inner man. Strengthen my faith to believe in Christ for a full share in His anointing. Day by day teach me to wait for and receive the anointing with fresh oil!

Father, help all your children to see that to abide in Christ we need the abiding anointing. We would walk humbly, in the dependence of faith, counting upon this anointing. Then will we be a sweet savor of Christ to all. Amen.

Personal Application

1. I think I know now the reason why at times we fail to abide. We read and study, listen and pray; we try to believe and strive to look to Jesus only, and yet we fail. What is missing is this: "His anointing teaches you about all things ... just as it has taught you, remain in him"; so far, and no farther.

2. The washing always precedes the anointing: we cannot have the anointing if we fail in the cleansing. When cleansed and anointed we are fit for His use.

3. Would you have the abiding anointing? Yield yourself wholly to be sanctified and made meet for the Master's use. Dwell in the holiest of all, in God's presence. Accept every chastisement as fellowship in the way of the rent flesh. Be confident the anointing will flow in union with Jesus. "It is like precious oil poured on the head ... running down on Aaron's beard, down upon the

collar of his robes" (Psalm 133:2).

4. The anointing is the divine eye salve, opening the eyes of the heart to know Jesus. So it teaches us to abide in Him. I am certain many Christians have no concept of the danger and deceitfulness of a religion that has its place only in the mind, with sweet and precious thoughts coming to us in books and preaching—and little power. The teaching of the Holy Spirit is in the heart *first;* man's teaching is in the mind. Let all our thinking lead us to cease from thought and to open our heart and will to the Spirit to teach us His own divine way, which is deeper than thought and feeling. Unseen, within the veil, the Holy Spirit abides. Be silent and still, believe and expect, and then cling to Jesus.

5. Oh, that God would visit His church and teach His children what it is to wait for and receive and walk in the full anointing, the anointing that abides and teaches to abide. Oh, that the truth of the personal leading of the Holy Spirit in every believer were restored in the church! He is doing it; He will continue to do it.

Chapter 31

Holiness and Heaven

*Since everything will be destroyed in this way, what kind of
people ought you to be? You ought to live holy and godly lives.*

2 Peter 3:11

*Make every effort . . . to be holy; without holiness
no one will see the Lord.*

Hebrews 12:14

*Let him who is holy continue to be holy. . . . The grace of the Lord
Jesus be with God's people. Amen.*

Revelation 22:11, 21

We are on our way to see God. We have been invited to meet the
Holy One face to face. The infinite mystery of holiness, the glory of
the invisible God, before whom the seraphim veil their faces, is to
be unveiled, revealed, to us. This is not something that we will
merely look into or study. No, we will actually see the Trinity, the
living God himself. God, the Holy One, will show himself to us. Oh,
the infinite grace and the inconceivable blessedness: we will see God!

All our schooling here in the life of holiness is simply the preparation for that meeting and that vision. We are to see God, the Holy One. "Blessed are the pure in heart, for they will see God" (Matthew 5:8). "Make every effort . . . to be holy; without holiness no one will see the Lord" (Hebrews 12:14). Since the time when God said to Israel, "Be holy, because I am holy" (Leviticus 11:44), holiness has been revealed as the only meeting place between God and His people. To be holy was the common ground on which to stand with Him. Holiness was the one attribute in which they were to be like God. To be holy was the one preparation for the glorious time when He would no longer need to keep them away, but would admit them to the full fellowship of His glory, to have the word fulfilled in them: "Let him who is holy continue to be holy" (Revelation 22:11).

In his second epistle, Peter reminds believers that the coming of the day of the Lord is to be preceded and accompanied by the most tremendous catastrophe—the dissolution of the heavens and the earth. He pleads with them to give diligence that they may be found without spot and blameless in His sight. He asks them to think seriously about what that coming day of the Lord will be and what it will bring, to consider what the life of those who look for such things ought to be: "What kind of people ought you to be? You ought to live holy and godly lives" (2 Peter 3:11). Holiness must be the one universal characteristic. At the close of our meditations on God's call to holiness and in the light of all that God has revealed of His holiness, and all that waits still to be revealed, we ask ourselves Peter's question "What kind of people ought you to be?"

Note first the meaning of the question. In the original Greek, the words *living* and *godliness* are plural. Alford says, "In holy behaviors and pieties, the plurals mark the holy behavior and piety in all its forms and examples." Peter would plead for a life of holiness pervading the whole man: our acts toward men and our worship and service toward God. True holiness cannot be found in anything less.

Holiness must be the one, the universal characteristic of our Christian life. In God we have seen that holiness is the central attribute, the comprehensive expression for divine perfection, the attribute of all the attributes, the all-including term by which He himself, as Redeemer and Father, His Son and His Spirit, His day, His house, His law, His servants, His people, His name, are marked and known. Always and in everything, in judgment as in mercy, in His exaltation and His condescension, in His hiddenness and His revelation, always and in everything God is the Holy One. And the Word would teach us that the reign of holiness, to be true and pleasing to God, must be supreme, must be in all holy living and godliness. There must not be a moment of the day or a relationship in life, nothing in the outer conduct or in the inmost recesses of the heart, nothing belonging to us whether in worship or in business that is not holy. The holiness of Jesus, the holiness that comes of the Spirit's anointing, must cover and pervade all. Nothing may be excluded if we are to be holy. It must be as Peter said when he spoke of God's call— holy in all manner of living. It must be as he says here: "You ought to live holy and godly lives." To use the significant language of the Holy Spirit, everything must be done in a way worthy of the saints, for God's holy people (Romans 16:2; Ephesians 5:3).

Note the force of the question "What kind of people ought you to be?" Peter says, "So then, dear friends, since you are looking forward to this, make every effort to be found spotless, blameless and at peace with him" (2 Peter 3:14). We have been studying through the course of Revelation the wonderful grace and patience with which God has made known and made us partakers of His holiness, all in preparation for what is to come. We have heard God the Holy One calling us, pleading with us, commanding us to be holy as He is holy. We expect to meet Him, to dwell through eternity in His light, holy as He is holy. It is not a dream. It is a living reality. We are looking forward to it as the one thing that makes life worth living. We are looking forward to love to welcome us, as with the confidence of childlike love we come as His holy ones to cry, "Holy Father!"

We have learned to know Jesus, the Holy One of God, our sanctification. We are living in Him day by day as those who are holy in Christ Jesus. We are drawing on His holiness without ceasing. We are walking in that will of God that He did and that He enables us to do. And we are looking forward to meeting Him with great joy: "On the day he comes to be glorified in his holy people and to be marveled at among all those who have believed" (2 Thessalonians 1:10). We have within us the Holy Spirit, the holiness of God in Christ come down to be at home within us as the earnest of our inheritance. He, the Spirit of holiness, is secretly transforming us within, sanctifying our spirit, soul, and body, to be blameless at His coming. He is making us meet for the inheritance of the holy ones in light. We are looking forward to the time when He shall have completed His work, when the body of Christ shall be perfected, and the bride, all filled and streaming with the life and glory of the Spirit within her, shall be set with Him on His throne, even as He sat with the Father on His throne. We hope through eternity to worship and adore the mystery of the Trinity. Even here it fills our souls with trembling joy and wonder. When God's work of making holy is complete, how we shall join in the song "Holy, holy, holy is the Lord God Almighty, who was, and is, and is to come" (Revelation 4:8).

In preparation for all this, the most wonderful events are to take place. The Lord Jesus himself will appear. The power of sin and the world will be destroyed. This visible system of things will be broken up. The power of the Spirit will triumph through all creation. There will be a new heaven and a new earth, wherein dwells righteousness. Then holiness will be unfolded in ever-growing blessedness and glory in the fellowship of the Trinity: "Let him who is holy continue to be holy." It is only necessary to ask the question for each believer to feel and acknowledge its force: "So then, dear friends, since you are looking forward to this. . . . What kind of people ought you to be? You ought to live holy and godly lives" (2 Peter 3:14, 11). Is such a question necessary? Can it be that God's holy ones—made holy in Christ Jesus, with the very spirit of holiness dwelling with them, on the way to meet the Holy One in His glory and love—need the question? It was needed in the time of Peter; it is all the more necessary in our day. How sad it is that there are so many Christians to whom the word *holy* is strange and unintelligible, even though it is the name by which the Father in His New Testament loves to call His children more than any other. There are many Christians for whom the word *holy* has little attraction because they have never seen that such a life is possible. It is even sadder how many there are, even workers in the Master's service, to whom "to live holy and godly lives" is a secret and a burden because they have not yet consented to give up all their will and their work for the Holy One to fill them with His Holy Spirit. Again the cry comes from those who do know the power of a holy life, lamenting their unfaithfulness and unbelief, as they see how much richer their entrance into the holy life might have been and how much fuller the blessing they still feel so unworthy to communicate to others. Peter's question is needed. Each one of us must answer it by the Holy Spirit through whom it came. Then we must pass it on to others that they and we may help one another in the faith and live in joy and hope.

Seeing that all these things will one day be dissolved, what manner of persons ought we to be in holy living and godliness? The time is short. The world is passing away. The heathen are perishing; Christians are sleeping. Satan is active and mighty. God's holy ones are the hope of the church and the world. What kind of people ought we to be? Shall we not seek to be such as the Father commands: holy, as He is holy? Shall we not yield ourselves afresh and undividedly to Him who is our sanctification, and to His blessed

Spirit, to make us holy in all our conduct and worship and service? Remembering the love of our Lord Jesus and the coming glory, in view of the coming end, of the need of the church and of the world, shall we not give ourselves to Him that we may have the power to bless each one we meet with the message of what God will do? Then it is possible that we might be a light and a blessing to this perishing world.

I close my study with the closing words of God's blessed Book: "He who testifies to these things says, 'Yes, I am coming soon.' Amen. Come, Lord Jesus. The grace of the Lord Jesus be with God's people. Amen" (Revelation 22:20–21).

Most Holy God! who has called us to be holy, we have heard your voice asking, "What manner of persons ought we to be in all holy living and godliness?" With our whole soul we answer in deep contrition and humility: "Holy Father! we ought to be so different from what we have been." In faith and love, in zeal and devotion, in Christlike humility and holiness, O Father! we have not been before you and the world what we ought to be, what we could be. We pray now for all who unite with us in this prayer and implore you to grant a great revival of true holiness in us and in all your church. We ask you to visit all ministers of your Word, that in view of your coming they may take up and sound abroad the question "What manner of persons ought we to be?" Lay upon them and all your people such a burden about the surrounding ungodliness and worldliness that they may not cease to cry to you. Grant them such a vision of the highway of holiness—the new and living way in Christ—that they may preach Christ our sanctification in the power and the joy of the Holy Spirit, with the confident and triumphant voice of witnesses who rejoice in what you do for them. O God, roll away the reproach of your people who, in spite of professing to be your people, have not been any humbler or holier, any more loving or any more heavenly than others.

Teach the world and us what manner of persons your people can be in the day of your power, in the beauty of holiness. O Father, we ask that you grant us, according to the riches of your glory, to be mightily strengthened in the inner man by your Spirit. Amen.

Personal Application

1. What manner of men ought you to be in all holy living? This is a question God has written down for us. Might it not help us if we were to write down the answer and say how holy we think we ought to be? The clearer and more distinct our views are of what God wishes, of what He has made possible, of what in reality ought to be, the more definite our acts of confession, of surrender, and of faith can become.

2. Let every believer who longs to be holy join in the daily prayer that God would visit His people with a great outpouring of the Spirit of holiness. Pray without ceasing that every believer may live as a holy one.

3. "Since you are looking forward to this . . ." Our life depends, in more than one sense, upon what we look at. "We fix our eyes not on what is seen." It is only as we look at the invisible and the spiritual, and come under its power, that we shall be what we ought to be in all holy living and godliness.

4. *Holy in Christ.* Let this be our parting word. However strong the branch becomes, however far away it reaches around the home, out of sight of the vine, all its beauty and all its fruitfulness depend upon that one point of contact where it grows out of the vine. May it be so with us. All the outer circumference of my life has its center in the ego—the living, conscious "I," in which my being roots itself. This "I" is rooted in Christ. Down in the depths of my inner life, there is Christ—holding, bearing, guid-

ing, quickening me into holiness and fruitfulness. In Him I am, in Him I will abide. His will and commands will I keep; His love and power will I trust. And I will daily seek to praise God that I am holy in Christ.